Lessons Learn

Table of Contents

Contents

Preface 3

Chapter 1 – Perfect Pretense 6

Chapter 2 – Fame and Glory 19

Chapter 3 – The American Dream 34

Chapter 4 – Dying in Paris 49

Chapter 5 – The Greeting Committee 64

Chapter 6 – Going Home 79

Chapter 7 – Reconstruction 93

Chapter 8 – Learning to Walk 107

Chapter 9 – Sharing the Story 122

Chapter 10 – Talking and Talking 136

Chapter 11 – Forget About It 150

Chapter 12 – My First Church 165

Chapter 13 – The Body of Christ 179

Chapter 14 – A Promise to Lydia 193

Chapter 15 – Loaves and Fish 209

Chapter 16 – God save the Church 224

Chapter 17 – Jesus is Life 239

Chapter 18 – Homesickness Please 254

Chapter 19 – Image of God 268

Chapter 20 – Call Upon the Name of the Lord 282

Lessons Learned

I dedicate this book to Marcia, my wife. She is the love of my life.

Lessons Learned

This book is my journey from unbelief to faith. I write about my inner struggles and, frankly, some of them are ugly. I'm ashamed of many things that I have done and pray that God will forgive me. I also pray that the people I have wounded will forgive me. There is no way to undo the harm that we have done, except to try to make amends and do better in the future. I am leaving out many of the details of my life experience because I want to focus on my spiritual journey and feel it's prudent to avoid vulgar and sensational specifics. It's not my intention to pander to peoples' prurient interests. Critics can find enough faults in me to dismiss me. I am simply a man trying to do the best with my abilities to comprehend things beyond my limitations. My hope is that my love of Jesus Christ will be the redeeming value of this testimony.

Every word in this book is true based upon my ability to know the truth. I take God seriously, and ultimately I'm aware that God knows what I am about. The day is coming when I'll die, and it will be the day I will be reunited with Jesus Christ. He knows all things, and He will look into my eyes at that time with His loving gaze. There is no deception or evasion possible before Him. I hope to hear him speak these words to me: "Well done good and faithful servant. Enter into my kingdom."

I have written this testimony so that we may share in the life Jesus offers us in this world and in the next. There are

Preface

This book is written for three persons. The first person is God. God is a mystery, but, one thing I know is that life is about loving our Creator. I try to please God, and the way to do that is to have that intention in all we do. The second person is Jesus Christ, whom I know intimately. More importantly Jesus knows me. I love Jesus and I want to share that love with everyone, so this book is all about discovering Jesus. The third person is the Holy Spirit who dwells in people. I hope and pray the Holy Spirit lives in you. There is only One God, and in God's self-revelation we have been given the understanding of knowing Him as three distinct persons.

The Bible teaches that God is love, and that is one lesson we are created to learn. I thought it would be so simple when Jesus taught me that lesson and sent me back to live it. I have since found it to be a lesson I am learning every day, and in many ways. Sometimes I fail miserably and others days there are victories. It is not about achieving perfection in this world; rather, it is all about striving for perfection. There is another time and place beyond this world where we will become perfect, and that is where Our Savior fits into the picture. I put my faith in Jesus Christ and He will complete what I cannot do.

Lessons Learned

many people who have known God better than I, and have lived lives far better than I've lived mine. I thank them for their example and fully acknowledge I would be lost without them. In ways that are often beyond my knowing, everyone I have met, and others I have never met, have contributed to my development. There is no way to list them all so I hope they will accept this simple statement of gratitude as sufficient. Every person is connected to all others in God's plan.

Thanks be to God for this gift of life that we have been given. Thank you, God, for the joys and the tears, for the light and the dark, for the pleasures and the pain, for the faith and the fears, for I know that "all things work together for good for those who love God, who are called to His purpose." Romans 8:28

As it is often said, "God is good, all the time!"

Lessons Learned

Chapter 1 – Perfect Pretense

Growing up in the suburbs of Boston in the nineteen forties and fifties was the American dream for us and many people like us. My father had returned from World War II, anxious to build a better life for his family after the interruption of serving in the United States Navy for several years in the South Pacific. My mother was raising two young daughters and one son by herself in a house far from her family. This was a world that was distinctly different from the world today.

My mother was raised to be absolutely compliant to her father and to any man. Against her will, she went to nursing school. As she was always submissive at home, she was always submissive to her husband. She didn't learn to drive a car until it was necessary in the mid nineteen fifties. We were furnished milk by the milkman in glass bottles. My mother would carefully pour the cream off the top of the milk and use it for special things. Vegetables came by a horse drawn wagon down the street. The tinker man, who sharpened knives and sold kitchen wares, was for unknown reasons to me, frightening to my mother, and she never patronized him. The Fuller brush man was considered a nuisance. There was a bakery truck which was filled with delights. The trash men came and emptied the trash can from the

Lessons Learned

street, and the garbage man came to the back of the house and emptied the garbage can that was set in the ground and covered with a heavy lid. We avoided the garbage man because he smelled bad. Every day there was something coming down our street, but the most exciting service (which only happened in the summertime) was the ice cream truck. It was completely unpredictable when it would appear, but the truck had a bell system that announced its arrival from a block away. The hope of being given a nickel to buy a frozen Popsicle was enough incentive to be in good favor with mother by doing what she asked.

Most of the neighbors were close in age so it was similar to growing up in a village. On weekdays all the men went to work early in the morning and didn't return until late in the day. The mothers supported each other in cooking and child care. Often we children were sent to a neighbor for a necessary missing ingredient for cooking. Everything was made from scratch and there were no frozen foods. Refrigerators had a freezer compartment that held two ice trays. In those years we had a wringer washing machine and mother hung the clothes on clotheslines in the back yard. The only other major electrical appliance my mother owned was a Hoover vacuum sweeper. She was very proud of her Hoover because there were other families not so fortunate to possess such a wonder-

Lessons Learned

working machine. The other electrical device our mother owned was her curling iron which she used almost every day to curl the ends of her hair. Her hair was an object of much pride in those days. If she went out of the house or someone came to the door her hair had to be fixed first. We loved that about her. It was really her only vanity. Having children, she had put on a lot of weight and wore shapeless plain dresses to hide her figure. I never saw her in anything other than a dress until she started wearing pants in her late seventies.

My mother and many other women of that era were totally devoted to raising their children, keeping an immaculate home, and being obedient to their husbands. Many families did not own an automobile. We were fortunate because my father was a traveling salesman and his company supplied him with a brand new Ford every year. When our father took our mother shopping once a week, we children got to carry the groceries from the car into the kitchen. We rarely were allowed to go on these shopping trips, and we learned it was forbidden to ask for anything at the store.

Our father was a mysterious figure in the house. His arrival home meant that we had to change our behavior. Everything had to be perfect for his arrival. My two sisters and I had to be clean and groomed. Our playtime was over when he appeared. Laughing, running, being silly and

Lessons Learned

acting like children was strictly forbidden in the house and anywhere else he might hear or see us. We were afraid of him because he had an explosive temper and freely administered slaps, kicks, and punches for both real and perceived infractions. He ran a tight ship, but we didn't know anything different and accepted it as our situation. We didn't understand what he did all day and on the rare occasions when we would complain to our mother, she invariably supported our father and told us to accept it.

Looking back, it isn't difficult to understand our father's behavior. He had been raised in an alcoholic home and his father lost everything in the great depression when he was a young man. He was struggling to be the financial success his father had failed to become. My father's mother was a converted Jew. My father was ashamed of his mother and was determined to prove he was a white, Anglo-Saxon, middleclass American. It's hard to imagine, unless you lived then, how much bigotry dominated life. Overt hatred for all immigrant groups, other denominations, religions different from your own, and differences in skin color were the norm and frequently the topic of general conversation in the most vulgar way. The irony of this contempt for everyone else was lost on these second-and-third generation "pure Americans". The culture of the time was totally materialistic and everyone we knew was striving to acquire wealth. Father worked

Lessons Learned

long days and nights and often on weekends at a job which he clearly found very stressful. Whatever fun my sisters and I had was when our father was not around, and when he was around we lived in fear of him.

In that culture, we believed everyone went to church on Sunday. That wasn't true, but it was what we thought. We never imagined someone wouldn't go to church on Sunday. Going to church was a big event because of the preparation. We had clothes that were for Sunday only and weren't worn at other times except funerals and weddings, which typically also happened in church. Going to church created lots of tension since we had to be properly attired and groomed. Children dressed like miniature adults. Women and girls wore white gloves and fancy hats. Men and boys wore suits, white shirts, and ties. We paraded from the car into church in birth order and in silence. There was no talking in church. Our only relief from the tedium of the church service was Sunday school which was usually separate from the worship service. Sunday school teachers were always women who did their best to engage us with Bible stories, songs, and craft projects. It was great fun and it was the only religious training my sisters and I received. There was no mention of religion in our home, except for derision of other religions.

Lessons Learned

We learned the Lord's Prayer and the Twenty-third Psalm in Sunday school. I accepted what was taught by our teachers, but had difficulty reconciling what we were taught with the reality we experienced at home. At church we were taught to be kind and to love all people, but at home we were told to despise anyone different from us and to have nothing to do with them. At church we were taught that love was kind and to not be angry. At home we experienced brutality and rage on a daily basis. There was a huge disconnect between what we were taught at church and what our daily experience of life was. As my sisters and I grew into adolescents we became disillusioned with the church because it appeared to us to be nothing but a weekly hour-long show that had no meaning in our lives. We exhibited perfect behavior in public and rode a roller coaster of emotions in private. Life was so unpredictable that my survival depended on withdrawing emotionally from everyone and everything. As time went on I became increasingly detached from those around me and lived in my own little world.

School was mostly fun and the teachers I had were really good people. The teachers liked me and, frankly, I adored them. My favorite subject was art and I became the class artist – privileged with special attention and favors. I had found a way to win attention from adults and was eager to be the best artist in class. My mother was an amateur

Lessons Learned

painter and encouraged me to paint. She helped me mix colors and I made my first oil painting at the age of nine. She even enrolled me in children's art classes at the Boston Museum of Fine arts on Saturdays. It was a wonderful experience, and there were times when I could wander through the museum and study the paintings. In addition to painting and drawing I became obsessed with Native American culture. On many days, after school, I would put on my Indian outfit and go off to the woods, pretending to be an Indian. I avoided people because I knew they would ridicule me if they saw me dressed as an Indian. There were times when I was convinced that I was destined to be an Indian and live a solitary life in the woods.

Around the age of ten my mother, sisters, and I were at the beach and I was swimming in water about three feet deep, which came up to my neck. I was with a boy I'd never seen before. He was several years older and much bigger than I, and after playing for a few minutes he pushed me under the water and held me there with his hands on my shoulders. I struggled to get free but couldn't. I hit his legs with my fists to make him release me, but hitting him had no effect. I stopped hitting him because I needed to breathe and knew that if I breathed the saltwater it would be bad. My lungs were begging for air since I'd expelled the air in my lungs yelling at him

Lessons Learned

underwater. I inhaled the seawater, looked up at the reflective underside of the surface, and suddenly saw what seemed to be sunlight radiating around me. I felt surrounded in brilliant white light and an absolute peace came over me. I remember going to sleep and being completely relaxed with the hands still holding me underwater. The next thing I remember is waking up on the beach with my mother straddled across my chest. She was both crying and pushing on my abdomen. I asked why she was crying and she pulled me up and hugged me very hard. I never saw that boy again and we never found out why he did that.

A couple of years later, when I was twelve, I found out that I had never been baptized. I asked our pastor if he would baptize me. At the time I was genuinely interested in having Jesus in my life and being a member of the church. Despite the disconnect between the church and our home life I wanted the love, joy, and peace that the church offered. I became active in the church youth program and was so enthusiastic that, when I was fourteen, the pastor told me he believed I had the call to be a minister. I was flattered but didn't think it was the life for me. By this time I was certain I was going to be an artist. I was taking scholarship art classes at the Decordova Museum of Art in Lincoln, Massachusetts, and I loved it! Our teachers were art students from the Boston

Lessons Learned

Museum of Fine Arts School. They were enthusiastic and encouraging. Being a budding artist in Junior High School and High School automatically made me a bit strange to my classmates.

When I began to read philosophy on my own there was no one to guide me, so I started with Plato and Aristotle. Soon I was reading whoever I could find in the library – philosophers like Kant and Nietzsche. I became very influenced by Nietzsche and then discovered the existentialists including Camus, Sartre, and Heidegger. I had moved into the popular world of atheism which was exciting because it supported the notion of needing no one and being independent of anybody, including God. This was the late nineteen fifties and early sixties when existentialism was quite fashionable. In those days, Time magazine had a cover story titled "God is Dead". None of my family was attending church at this time except me. I was in the church youth group which was led by my pastor. I called and asked him if he and I could talk. He agreed and I asked him many theological questions. He confided that he didn't believe in heaven or hell or the divinity of Jesus, or angels, or anything supernatural. After that conversation I stopped attending church because there was no point in it. He confirmed my suspicions that church was just a show based on traditions that nobody

Lessons Learned

believed in. I didn't attend any church for the next twenty-three years.

There was something else going on in my life at that time which can be characterized in one word: hormones. I was going girl crazy. The culture of the time was becoming openly sexual. Popular music was all about romance and often alluded to sex. Rock and roll of the early sixties was not very subtle about the underlying message. When Jerry Lee Lewis screamed, "great balls of fire", teenage boys got the message. To adolescents, the message was clear: if you want to feel love, engage in sex. So for many, love became equated with sex. I definitely wanted to love and be loved so I went in hot pursuit of like-minded members of the opposite sex. Record companies made millions of dollars and young musicians became millionaires overnight. Unfortunately a generation was corrupted by the message, which is a lie, but it was very attractive to adolescents. This was one of several forces that captured the baby boom generation and tossed faith in God out of our culture. At that time, my generation embraced hedonism with heart, mind, and soul. Many of this generation, possibly millions, became hedonists/nihilists/atheists. There were powerful factors such as the threat of total nuclear war, frustration with the slow progress of the civil rights movement, the disastrous Vietnam War, the assassination of esteemed

Lessons Learned

leaders, and the moral bankruptcy of the materialistic culture. This was the cultural wave we were riding which was leading us to drugs.

Leaders emerged to encourage this "dawning of a new age" – people like Timothy Leary, Owsley, and Charley Manson, to name a few. Many of us, the "baby boomers", bought into this, hook, line, and sinker. By this time I'd had a wife and daughter and we moved to San Francisco. We were eighteen when we'd married in 1966 and heard that San Francisco was the place to be. We went there and thought we were in the middle of a cultural revolution. It was exciting and captivating, but mostly delusional. I was attending the San Francisco Art Institute full time and working full time at night waiting on tables in a restaurant to pay for school. I never had time to be a hippie, but many of our friends were fully involved in the drug culture. It was frightening to witness people come to San Francisco from good homes in the East and go completely wild. They would become extremely promiscuous and get high on drugs all the time. We would see them lose any sense of hygiene and morality and within a few weeks or months they would become incapable of rational thought or conversation – living for the next high. It was very disturbing to watch this happen repeatedly to people who'd been our friends. We ultimately lost them as friends because we would suggest

Lessons Learned

that they were falling apart and they'd just turn on us and go away. There were many lost souls who did things that I'm certain they deeply regret today. Mercifully the whole disaster burned itself out in a few years. In San Francisco we knew it was over in 1968. It took a while for the rest of the country to realize it was over.

Working full time at a restaurant five days a week from ten at night 'til four-thirty or five in the morning, and taking eighteen to twenty-two credit hours of course work, left me very little time to sleep. There was no time for drugs or play. Married with a child, it was too risky to fool around with illegal drugs. We tried a few things but never were very interested. My goal was to get my undergraduate degree, which I did in two and a half years, and then attend graduate school so that I could find a college teaching position in art. I went to the University of California Berkeley across the San Francisco Bay because it was a good school and I could afford the in-state tuition. My life was driven by the desire to get the degrees required to be a college art professor. After the fiasco of the "cultural revolution" there was a turning-away from the hippie thing and, like so many, I was becoming career conscious and seeking a way to make a living.

Lessons Learned

Lessons learned

1. Our parents are the first influencers of our lives. By their examples and words they shape our behaviors and values. Our understanding of God is one of the most important responsibilities of parents.

2. Adolescence is a distressing time for many children. Too often the dysfunctional dynamics of the family lead a child into rebellion and rejection of cultural standards. Due to these situations, this rebellious stage is often expressed as rejection of the church and alienation from God.

3. There are competing influences in our culture to support values contrary to Christian morality. Some of these influences are powerful and compelling. In American society it's impossible to shield our youth from these forces.

4. A strong relationship with Jesus Christ is the only foundation that can protect our youth. When this is lost it is most difficult to regain it because of the counterfeit gods of the world.

5. Hypocrisy in the church has diminished faith for innumerable people. Authentic belief in God cannot be replaced by allegiance to ritual, strict dogma, social justice issues, or blind obedience. Authentic faith is an experience of God that is personal and contagious.

Lessons Learned

Chapter 2 – Fame and Glory

Famous artists were well known for enormous egos. This was true in all the arts and one rarely heard about a humble artist. We art students didn't talk about the meek artist; rather we admired the really grandiose egotists. There was a common assumption that if you weren't consumed by your art, you were not really dedicated and you would never be great. Greatness was the driving force. Someday there would be a large monograph on your work with your name printed on the back spine. People would come from around the world to purchase your work. Museums would compete to exhibit your paintings. That was the dream. To be rich and famous was secretly our motivation, but we were too "cool" to openly admit it.

The art world had long ago stopped supporting religious art, narrative art, or art that communicated to ordinary people. Art was now about cults of personality and always-changing new fads. So fame in the art world became fleeting and changed year after year. The most important goal for an artist was to do something shocking and different. Art had become an investment for the super-rich and they were advised by art critics who controlled the medium of art publications. Artists had become pawns in the game of wealth management.

Lessons Learned

Someone would be "hot" one year and the next year they would be forgotten. The good thing about becoming a teacher was that it provided a steady income and security. Naturally, the artists who were struggling to sell enough work to live on held the teaching artist in contempt for being a sellout to the middle-class. My wife was clear about not accepting an artist's lot, starving for the sake of my genius. That was a disappointment, but not unreasonable. "Live hard, die young" was our motto. I completed my Master's degree in one year and got accepted into the masters of Fine Arts program, which was the terminal degree in painting. I had applied for an artist-in-residence program in Roswell, New Mexico. To my delight and surprise I was accepted for a one year residency. The only thing I knew about the program was that it was in the desert. Our son was born in December and in January 1970 we traveled with our belongings to Roswell. We were given a house to live in, a huge studio to paint in, and a generous monthly stipend. The only condition was to have an exhibition of work at the end of the year. This was a dream come true. I worked in my studio twelve to fourteen hours a day, seven days a week. That year I completed seventy six paintings. We were living on the edge of the desert and it was very beautiful. We learned that people either love the desert or they hate it – that it is similar to living next to the sea. The light and the openness are unlike anywhere else. My paintings

Lessons Learned

were mostly landscapes of the desert. At the exhibition of my work at the Roswell Museum a number of paintings sold which provided income to return to Berkeley and school.

When I showed my desert paintings in Berkeley it was evident that people didn't appreciate them. The bleakness and simplicity of the landscapes didn't interest them. I knew it was good work, but most people couldn't relate to it. I was consumed with my painting and had no time or interest in anything else, but now I had to complete the MFA degree requirements and find a job teaching in a college anywhere I could find one. It was painful leaving the San Francisco Bay area because it is so beautiful and we had many good friends there, but I had to go where I could find work at a University.

I was hired by a state college in Kentucky that was just getting started in a suburb south of Cincinnati, Ohio. This seemed to be a great opportunity to build an art program. The college hired over eighty new faculty that year which was the majority of the teaching staff. The people that were hired were similar in age, background, and attitudes. The administrators were older Kentucky staff who were conservative and distrustful of the new, young, radicals arriving from outside Kentucky. It created tensions that eventually led to turmoil and firing of some of the perceived "troublemakers". Somehow I was accepted by

Lessons Learned

both groups and was asked to lead the art department my second year. So at the age of twenty five I became a tenured professor at a rapidly growing university. It was exhilarating teaching classes, trying to administer an art department, paint my own art, plan for the future of the program, and fight the battles! The best part of it all was the delightful students. The students were not particularly sophisticated, but they were eager to learn. Most of the students were the first generation in their families to attend college. Since art was an elective, we only had students that were interested and motivated. Some of the students were veterans from the Vietnam War, some were veteran teachers, and others were homemakers now free to explore a passion for art. These were young people looking for direction in their lives. I loved teaching them about art.

From 1972 to 1985 I taught hundreds of students all levels of drawing, all levels of painting, design, and art appreciation. The content of the courses was competently covered in my classes. But the students are influenced by their teachers in ways beyond the specific course content, ways which are sometimes subtle and at other times overt. Since Northern Kentucky University was a state school there was an implied understanding that religion was not part of the curriculum. In reality, many professors stated their religious understandings directly and

Lessons Learned

indirectly in the teaching of their various subjects. Most of the faculty members that I knew were atheists, and they held Christianity in contempt. In the process of teaching, these views would be made known to the students. Ridicule, sarcasm, and mockery were most often used as the means for expressing this attitude of intellectual superiority, denigrating Christianity. This was completely acceptable behavior in academia. In a world where freedom of expression was supposedly the highest code of behavior, on one hand, professors were free to deride Christianity while, on the other hand, they were prohibited to speak positively about it. The Christian professors I knew never spoke about their faith in the classroom. After my conversion to Christianity in 1985, the Dean of the College of Arts and Science told me in his office that I was never to talk about God, Christ, or the Bible in my classes. There had never been a complaint about my doing this because I had never done so; he was just concerned that I might do that in the future. He patiently explained to me that as a state school we must respect the separation of church and state.

One of my regrets in life is that I sat there and agreed to not commit this offense because it would somehow be contrary to the constitution of the United States of America. How many people have been fed this lie and accepted it as truth? How many impressionable young

Lessons Learned

people have caught the cynicism of their professors and mistaken it as intellectual truth? The attractive quality of being a cynic is that a person makes a belief system out of denying other belief systems. There is no ground of belief in cynicism other than contempt for other beliefs. One can argue endlessly against things as long as one has nothing to defend. To be fair in this assessment of cynical professors, it must be pointed out that they believed in materialism. For them the only reality was that which is observable. Of course, this leaves no room for abstract notions like love, hope and faith. No one can exist in the world for even an hour without love, hope and faith in something, yet a cynic might deny these as simple delusions necessary for survival. These are learned instinctive responses to a meaningless and random existence. From this, interspersed into the curriculum of whatever subject was being taught, was bashing of Christianity. How many impressionable young minds were infected with this philosophy of despair? How many young people came to the university with a church background and became convinced they had been deceived into believing fairy tales and superstition? They certainly learned that a person of superior intellect had no use for faith in anything that was not scientifically observable. To my everlasting shame I participated in this travesty of intellectual freedom.

Lessons Learned

There is no prohibition in the United States Constitution against teaching Christianity. The constitution prohibits establishment of a state church. The founding fathers didn't want a state church like there was in the European countries. They wanted freedom of religious practice and never envisioned a prohibition against religion. That's how atheists have promoted their agenda and deceived even Christians into thinking freedom of religion is absence of religion. In fact, it's not absence of religion that's practiced; rather, it's an assault on religion, and specifically Christianity. For thirteen of the twenty years I was a professor at a state university I was an atheist and openly preached atheism in my classes. During the last seven of those years, I was a Christian and kept silent about my faith while in the classroom. Looking back, I was wrong to do this. Academic freedom allowed me to openly express my faith and I should have expressed it when it was relevant to the content or class discussion. In art there are many opportunities to discuss the faith of the artist. What a disservice it is to the meaningful exploration of art to ignore or ridicule the religious basis for the art being discussed. How many people know that Vincent Van Gogh was a devout Christian and served for a time as a Christian missionary? The examples are endless. We have a university level education system that pretends to be devoid of religion while openly allowing attacks on Christianity. If you find this hard to believe, ask

Lessons Learned

students who have had professors who have gone out of their way to repudiate Christian faith.

Before I became a Christian, a woman who had been in my classes for several years came to see me. She told me her brother was considering becoming a Catholic priest. She had tried to get him to talk to me because she knew I could convince him not to do it. Years later, after I became a Christian, I asked her what had happened to him, and she told me he became a priest. I told her "Thank God he never talked to me!" A few years after that incident I was speaking at a Catholic church and the young priest of that parish approached me after the talk. He identified himself and confirmed the story I just related. I told him I was thankful to God he refused to speak with me back then. He said he was, too.

After my conversion, my family never went to church. The only religion they'd ever been exposed to was Christian bashing at home. It's impossible for me to express how deeply I regret raising my son and daughter this way. If it were not for the forgiveness of sin that Christ gives when we repent, I couldn't live with this sin. It has had an irreparable impact on my relationship with both my son and daughter. Because I don't wish to alienate them more than I have already, I can't discuss this further. If you were to assume the worst, your impression is probably close to the truth. This is very painful for me. I have no way of

Lessons Learned

knowing what they believe. They were teenagers when I had my conversion to Christ Jesus. Every time I hear people say that they don't take their children to church so that they can make up their own minds about religion as adults, I am appalled. Exposure to faith is not only important it is essential! Would you send someone you cared about into the wilderness without a map or directions? Sometime in their lives, our children will be exposed to faith in materialism, atheism, hedonism, and Satanism. So why are we afraid of exposure to Jesus Christ?

We are afraid of Jesus Christ because He might be exactly who He said He was. When I was an atheist I would never admit I was afraid of Jesus. I avoided any mention of Him except to ridicule him. In the core of my being there was an emptiness that haunted me every day. I tried everything I could think of to fill this void in my soul. I tried alcohol to anesthetize myself. This was the drug of choice of my professor friends. We drank lots of booze. Some were alcoholics and the rest of us frequently drank to excess. It didn't help with the problem except to pollute the mind and spirit enough to not deal with that emptiness for a few hours. I was a sex addict, addicted to pornography. The excuse for that was, "It doesn't harm anyone." That is a lie. It harms the people who make the garbage and it harms viewers because they fixate on

Lessons Learned

illusions and miss the relationships close to them. I craved approval in fame and fortune. Those never satisfy because there is never enough fame and fortune. One of the bitterest men I ever knew was an artist who had been very famous for a few years. It was frightening to see how angry and bitter he became over not being more famous and wealthy. I tried being an egotist. The problem with making yourself a god is that unless you're psychotic, it's impossible to convince yourself by your act. We're afraid of Jesus because He might show us the truth of who we are. We are scared to death of condemnation and damnation. We don't know what Jesus would do if we let Him into our lives, but we keep Him away out of fear of what we imagine He would do.

Who Jesus is and what He would do with us, if we really knew Him, is a mystery to most of the world. Is it not strange that Jesus is unknown and not spoken of at most colleges and universities, and yet they're called places of higher learning? Why is learning about the Christian faith generally prohibited in public schools? How can a person resist the temptations of a self-destructive lifestyle when they have no foundation in a Higher Power? The most successful program to help people achieve sobriety begins with the step of acknowledging powerlessness against addiction and learning to rely upon a Higher Power. As long as people are suffering with emptiness in their souls,

Lessons Learned

they are doomed to addiction of some kind. These addictions are false gods who promise happiness but deliver misery. Who do you think is behind that program?

Millions of people alive today can testify to the power of God to help them and heal them. I have learned through personal experience that direct access to God is through God's revelation of His nature in the person of Jesus Christ. This is the very reason the attack on God is directed at Jesus and His church. In academia and in much of the world, it's acceptable to discuss esoteric philosophies and religions as speculations. There are vast numbers of books, programs and groups devoted to spiritual development, but as long as they're not connected to Christianity they're tolerated and often supported. When I was a pagan artist I dabbled in the psychic arts and had some experiences that were startling. For example, one time I was carving a life-size figure and hadn't been able to connect its likeness to anyone. On a whim, I asked the walnut log for its name. It spoke to me and said, "Menelaus." I didn't recognize the name, but remembered it and asked a history professor. He immediately recognized the name and told me about the person with that name in one of Homer's poems. There were several occasions when I spoke to wood carvings, and they would answer me. I felt it was

Lessons Learned

acceptable to explore the psychic world as long as it didn't involve God.

Many of my carvings were about Greek gods, and they always elicited a very positive response. Although I considered myself a painter I won an award as Kentucky Sculptor of the Year from the Kentucky Arts Council, which included a significant cash award. During this time I was becoming obsessed with a huge dead ash tree located at the bottom of the hill in my backyard. It had once contained a large tree house I had built for my son. Every time I looked at it I saw the image of Jesus crucified. This image became clearer over a period of a several years, but I thought to myself I was not going to carve Jesus. Why would I do such a crazy thing? I also knew I would be subjecting myself to ridicule for carving Jesus.

I fought the impulse to carve Jesus for years until one day I knew it was not going to stop calling me until I did it. The first problem was that this tree was huge and it was about seventy five yards down a very steep hill. I cut the tree down, wrapped a chain around it, and used a pulley at the top to pull it up the hill to the back of my house. It took a whole day of exhausting work. This was going to be a life-size figure, and the outstretched arms of Christ were the massive branches. Carvings of this size take two to three months to complete, but I completed a realistic carving of the crucified Christ in a little over two weeks. I couldn't

Lessons Learned

stop working on it and could see it perfectly in the log. I made a cross out of old four-by-fours and bolted Jesus to the cross by his hands and feet. Stains in the ash wood developed as tears and blood stains in the appropriate places. Some might presume I had stained the wood, but these were naturally occurring stains in the wood. The entire time I worked on the carving I was under a compulsion to complete it, and when it was finished I had no idea what to do with it.

There was soon to be an art faculty exhibition, so I put it in the university gallery along with a couple of other pieces. This ten-foot-tall sculpture was met with complete silence by my colleagues, which surprised me. A few students told me they liked it. When I brought it home I knew I had to do something with it, so I called a former student who was a nun. When she saw it she said she knew someone who might want it. She called a priest who was a chaplain at a federal prison in Kentucky. When he saw it he said he wanted it for the prison chapel. A few days later a pickup truck from the prison arrived to take it away. I was relieved to have it out of my home because it disturbed me every time I was near it. It would draw me in, but I'd resist its strange attraction. I'd say to it, "I don't believe in you." The stains in the pale ash wood got deeper in color over time. I think it still hangs in that prison.

Lessons Learned

My wife and children asked me why I carved Jesus and I told them I didn't know. It wasn't something I understood or wanted to think about. I was eager to give people elaborate explanations about other carvings but didn't want to speak about Jesus. In 1985 when I met Jesus, I asked Him why I never knew Him before. He explained to me that He had reached out to me many times and I had always rejected Him. I wept when Jesus told me this.

Lessons Learned

Lessons Learned

1. It's an advantage in life to have a passion for something that can provide a living. Striving for success is a good motivation, but when a person losses their soul the passion becomes a monster which is never satisfied.
2. Every profession has its own culture, and to be successful in the profession one must adapt to the prevailing culture. The secular side of our culture dominates education and has driven God and religion out of many of the young people it serves.
3. Our faith influences people we work with, people we work for, and everyone we contact. Faith can't totally be a private matter because it colors everything we do. A natural question, therefore, is, how should Christians show their faith in the secular world we work in?
4. Atheists dominate every aspect of our society, and the battle for hearts and minds is being lost by Christians. What is the appropriate response of Christians to this struggle?
5. Jesus is faithful even when we are not. Statistically, the majority of Americans are Christian, but their influence on our culture is rapidly disappearing. We are becoming a pagan society.

Chapter 3 – The American Dream

When we were in our early twenties we never thought we would live to reach our thirties. The ever present threat of global annihilation from a nuclear war between the Soviet Union and the United States appeared to be imminent. There was a group of scientists who had a clock set at almost midnight signifying nuclear war was seconds away. A movie, "On the Beach" realistically portrayed the last days of the few remaining people dying. Everyone I knew expected the world to end at any time by hydrogen bombs, with radiation spreading around the globe. The interest in bomb shelters had ended in the early sixties because people realized they might survive the initial blasts of a nuclear exchange, but eventually no one would survive the fallout. During the Cuban missile crisis I was living with a woman in New York City, and we were glued to a radio fully expecting the end of life at any minute. A high school friend of mine told me later he was in the Atlantic Ocean on a nuclear submarine during the Cuban missile crisis and the entire crew was certain they were going to launch their H-bomb-tipped missiles at any moment. They literally had their fingers on the trigger. Fear of the end of the world at any moment was not illusion; it was an ongoing reality. It's not surprising that a

Lessons Learned

generation turned to hedonism and immediate gratification.

From today's perspective it's almost impossible to understand the fear and hatred of communism at that time. The world was divided between two incompatible systems, and only one was going to prevail. The problem was that the hatred and fear was so intense on both sides that it seemed there would be mutually assured destruction of everyone. Both sides had enough nuclear weapons, with the capacity to deliver them, to annihilate the entire world several times over. Many believed we needed to eat, drink, and be merry for tomorrow we'd die. Most people went about their daily lives with this threat hanging over their heads; others just dropped out and did their own thing. When the generation that had fought in World War II came home they worked hard to build a better life for themselves and their families. They succeeded in surpassing their parents in wealth accumulation and material progress. The next generation, who were their children, was a huge disappointment to them. Much of what they'd valued was rejected by their children. The two generations were locked in a combat of values.

My father and I had almost no relationship. He had told me that I was the biggest disappointment of his life, and he meant it. I had no respect for him and barely tolerated

Lessons Learned

him, just so that I could have some interaction with my mother. My parents lived in Massachusetts and I lived in California. That was as far away as I could get from my father. We rarely spoke or saw each other. My father was contemptuous of art and considered my becoming an artist equivalent to becoming a bum. He was quite vocal about that. There was nothing about my father I admired.

When I was twelve years old I asked for a set of weights for Christmas. I wanted to build my muscles so that I could defend myself against the frequent blows from my father. I lifted weights every day for an hour or two. By the age of fourteen I was six feet two inches tall and had become quite strong. I was playing football and throwing the shot put and the discus in track. One day my father exploded in rage about something and came towards me with his fist raised to strike. Rather than standing there and being punched, I put my fists up and moved toward him. He began to back up so I moved toward him. He backed up more and I keep moving in on him. He panicked and began to run away and I chased him around the house. I could have caught him but it was satisfying to just have him run from me. He never hit me again after that. From that time on I became more emotionally independent of him. Sometimes he would be raging at me and I would walk away from him to show him my contempt. When I was fifteen I ran away from home and

Lessons Learned

lived in New York City for four months. I found that I could do whatever I wanted to do and no one was going to stop me. At one point my father tried to get me committed to a mental institution, but I took off back to New York and he didn't try it again.

When I came home from being away for months he demanded I see a psychiatrist which I was willing to do. By the grace of God I was sent to a man who primarily worked with Harvard students. He was wonderful, and we became friends as much as that is possible between a doctor and patient. This kind man helped me develop strategies for survival in my dysfunctional family. He helped me clarify my thinking and see things more realistically. It's unfortunate that everyone doesn't have access to a therapist. If I could afford it I would continue to make therapy a regular part of my life. Instead, I've made a regular habit of belonging to peer groups that have a therapeutic component. Later I'll discuss how a therapeutic group saved my life. Socrates said, "The unexamined life is not worth living." That is how I see life. There are so many people who appear to lack insight into themselves. They keep doing the same things over and over and expect to get different results.

As I moved from college student to university professor I became more and more confident of my power and even had feelings of superiority. Being stronger and smarter

Lessons Learned

than most people, I became more arrogant and full of myself. As an artist and art teacher, this act worked very well for me. In my family this was becoming precariously similar to the tyranny of my father which horrified me. When I would become angry with my wife and children, it scared me. I restrained myself from physical violence toward them, but I certainly was threatening, and they felt it. I'm sure they resent me for that to this day. I wish I had been a better husband and father, but I was doing what worked for me at the time. Without the help of God, it's almost impossible to change yourself. After my conversion I have come to rely on the power of God to make changes in myself.

My father used to say there are two kinds of people; takers and givers. I would modify that to users and givers. True humility is to put others' needs ahead of your own. Users see others as an opportunity to get something they want. Everyone has both of these impulses going on in their minds, but no one is predetermined to live as one extreme or the other. What makes the critical difference is self-awareness of the choices and the desire to make the better choice. With the Holy Spirit absent from your life, there is little motivation for being compassionate. Most of life is survival mode. What is defined as love in our culture is largely gratification of the ego. As an atheist I considered myself a good person, but I was the sole

Lessons Learned

judge of what was good. I invented my own standards to suit my desires. This may work well for individuals, but not necessarily for people around them. Those I associated with considered themselves good people. Just as I did, they defined for themselves what was good and created their own standards.

Within my group of associates, we cared about each other, shared laughter and pleasures, and concentrated on raising our families and pursuing careers. We had transitioned from the chaos of the nineteen-sixties into lives that looked very much like the lives of our parents. The difference was that we were intellectuals and our parents were not. We had a sense of intellectual superiority to the rest of the world. Being highly educated in our specific disciplines made us authorities in our fields of expertise, and this was the foundation for our sense of elitism. Teaching young adults subjects from this perspective led to an even greater sense of grandeur. The ego was out of control. We were paid more than public school teachers, but not what other professionals made. Our incomes were sufficient to be comfortably middle class. The University had excellent health benefits and retirement and our security was ensured once we had tenure. This was the American dream fulfilled.

With all the comforts of life amply supplied, what more could we have possibly wanted? Our hope was that our

Lessons Learned

children would go to good colleges and have successful careers, marry well, and raise families. The cycle of life would continue as it seemed to have from the beginning of time. Each generation dreamed that the next generation would progress forward in well-being. All of us had heard about the poverty of the Great Depression of the nineteen-thirties but we had distanced ourselves from that time of scarcity to a culture of material abundance. The previous generations that had gone to church and prayed daily had a faith that was not passed on to their children. What exposure to God we had received had been rejected as nonsense. It's normal for people to put their faith, hope, trust, and belief in something, and we put our faith in the idols we created. The notion that we were self-created and knew the measure of all things was our underling belief system. We thought the successes in our lives validated this arrogance.

The culture of the nineteen-sixties, seventies, eighties, and nineties was supportive of this world view. How much the culture led in this direction or followed the trends by pandering to hedonism is arguable. The answer is that likely both are true. Americans began leaving the church in the early sixties. The decline in church attendance dropped precipitously for the next few decades. Hollywood stopped making movies with religious themes. Clergy became objects of ridicule on television and in

Lessons Learned

movies as opposed to being portrayed as heroic figures a generation earlier. Displays of religious thought such as prayer, nativity scenes, and Biblical quotes became prohibited. It was open season on Christianity in the United States of America. This was upsetting to the remnant of Christians, but they had been marginalized and had little influence. The majority of Americans were indifferent or hostile to Christianity. Thousands of churches closed every year, a trend that continues to this day. A few new churches opened, but the statistics confirmed an overall decline in church attendance of approximately one percent per year. Christianity in Europe declined even more rapidly. All indications showed Christianity becoming extinct in a few decades. Along with that expected demise was a rapid growth in occult beliefs. Bookstores added New Age sections that were often larger than religion sections. Self-help books proliferated, offering every form of "spiritual" courses. New age gurus introduced reworked forms of reincarnation, channeled masters, astral projection, spiritual mastery, and other commodities of advancement to win the hearts and minds of devotees. It seemed there was a new cult emerging every month.

A professor in the art department became involved in a new cult from Japan. He became heavily immersed in it and was soon promoting it to his students and anyone

Lessons Learned

who would listen. He got another member of the art faculty involved and soon they were having meetings on campus and off campus. The complaints and comments started trickling into my office. I had been a member of the art faculty for twenty years and department head for seven and a half years. When I challenged them about proselytizing their religion in the classroom they had a variety of defenses. They claimed they were only helping students develop by teaching them spiritual practices. They said they weren't forcing the students to accept their beliefs. They also asserted that they were within their rights, practicing freedom of speech and religion. They continued teaching their occult ideas in spite of being advised not to engage in this activity. Both professors left the university to devote all of their time and energy to furthering their new religion. The rest of us considered them crazy, but no one doubted their sincerity. They weren't forced out or oppressed in any way by the rest of us. They each had tumultuous marital problems and serious health problems. The chaos in their personal lives contrasted with their claims of healing and great inner peace. I haven't heard anything about their cult in many years. Someone else that I knew was always excited about some seminar they'd attended. In the following years friends often gave away books from the latest channeled master, and there was regularly the latest guru in town giving a presentation they believed I

Lessons Learned

should attend. I looked at some of these things but was never impressed.

No Christian ever invited me to church in my adult life. No one ever handed me a tract or a Bible. No one ever spoke about Jesus to me. During good weather our campus was visited by evangelists. They met on a lawn that was near the entrance to the art building and would scream insults at the students and damn them to hell. Most people avoided them, but there were always a few students who would engage them by hurling insults back at them. There were shouting matches of insults. I found them disgusting and wondered about the sanity of these evangelists. Their approach was so confrontational it appeared to be counterproductive. I don't know how many converts they won, but I know that many of the students and faculty found them to be extremely unappealing. How much good they did for faith in Jesus Christ I don't know, but I'm well aware of how much harm they did by turning us away from Christianity. After my conversion, I found Christians on the campus and discovered that they had kept their faith invisible to the rest of us.

The only time we heard about Christians on television was during a scandal. A pastor or priest would do something horrible and that would make the news. Thousands of decent Christians working for the poor or risking their lives in foreign missions were never noticed. Considering

Lessons Learned

the thousands of Christians involved with good works, it's strange that none of this was ever given any notice considering that there were often news stories about a child who had raised money for a sister with cancer, or a fireman who had rescued a dog from a burning building. Apparently feeding hundreds of poor everyday or caring for the homeless wasn't newsworthy. There was a conspiracy to keep Christianity out of the public eye.

My one brush with a Christian happened in 1973. I was teaching a summer painting class and a nun in a habit enrolled in the class. Her name was Sister Dolores, and she was a high school teacher in a nearby Catholic school. When the first class was over, I asked to speak with her privately. I told her that I was an atheist and I did not allow any talk of religion in my classroom. She assured me that was not a problem. She said she was there to learn how to paint. Soon I discovered she was a talented painter and very eager to learn. We became friends because of her interest in art. I never could understand how she didn't get paint on her black habit. She was always immaculate. She had a delightful personality and was quick to laugh. When the class was over I missed her company. I am sure I was drawn to her for reasons I didn't know. As time went on she would invite me to come to her high school to give art lectures. This was an opportunity to maintain our friendship for me. She also

Lessons Learned

sent me Christmas and Easter cards and would conclude them with a note stating she was praying for me. I had no idea what that meant and assumed it was some kind of "best wishes" closing. It wasn't until after my conversion that I discovered that she was a large part of the reason I was alive and had been reborn into faith in Christ Jesus.

— — — — — — — — —

After my near death experience June 1st 1985 and after the first periods of hospitalization, I was at home rehabilitating so that I would become strong enough for additional surgery. There had been major surgery in France followed by a couple months of care in a hospital in Kentucky. I was very weak and felt that I was literally coming back from the dead. I wanted to talk with a Christian but I knew only one person whom I thought would understand what I had to say. I wasn't interested in talking about religion; rather, I wanted to talk about Jesus whom I had met. I remembered Sister Dolores and called her. I invited her to visit me explaining that I was too ill to leave the house.

She sat opposite me in a rocking chair while I told her what happened for well over an hour. At that time I was so emotionally close to the experience of dying and meeting Jesus that I could barely speak. Mostly I'd weep for long periods, say a few words, and then weep some

Lessons Learned

more. Sister Dolores sat patiently and listened to me. I was aware that this was wearing on her. When I finished, she said she would come back when I was feeling better. I begged her to come back and apologized for crying so much. She came back a week later and I repeated my testimony of meeting Jesus, but this time I tried to be more composed and cry less. She sat perfectly still and listened to me without interruption. After close to two hours I had completed my testimony. I asked her if she had any questions. She said, "I have one question. Why did it take so long?"

"What do you mean?" I asked.

"I have been praying for you for thirteen years, and I wonder why it took so long. The sisters in the convent have been praying for you as well. We have been praying every day for thirteen years for you," she said.

I started crying and couldn't stop. I felt then that this was one of the reasons I had been rescued from death and given a new life in Christ. My friend, this nun, had been praying for me and had never given up. I love my friend Sister Dolores and will be eternally grateful for her faith in God and her persistence in prayer. We see each other occasionally and she is still someone I admire very much. I believe that sister Dolores was sent by God to intercede for me so I would be saved from destruction. So often

Lessons Learned

people ask what they can do to serve God; what Sister Dolores did for me, anyone can do for someone else – namely, care about and pray for them. Sister cared enough to maintain a relationship over so many years in spite of the fact that I was antagonistic to everything she believed in as a Catholic. She cared enough to pray every day for me for thirteen years before, as she would tell you, she had her prayers answered! She cared enough to ask others to pray for someone they didn't know. She cared enough to have the courage of faith. Thank God for people like her!

Lessons Learned

Lessons Learned

1. The post World War II baby boomers were frequently confronted with an expected and sudden annihilation by nuclear war. This challenged all traditional beliefs and led to many becoming nihilists, materialists, hedonists, and having other world views.
2. Many Americans, the wealthiest, freest and most prosperous people in the world, went adrift in pursuit of something meaningful. Christianity was competing for souls along with numerous other beliefs. Christian evangelism was too often ineffective and anti-intellectual.
3. In the past sixty years Christianity has been demeaned in the popular media of music, movies, news, magazines, books, and television. Today, it's rare to see positive representations of Christianity.
4. One person of faith can make all the difference in the life of another. The prayers of a faithful person can change the course of a non-believer and save their soul.
5. In our American society which can be overtly hostile to faith in God, how do we evangelize effectively? Do we know someone who needs a relationship with Jesus Christ? A natural question for the Christian is, just who are we to pray for?

Chapter 4 – Dying in Paris

Paris is one of the most beautiful cities in the world. Everyone should see Paris if possible. I had always wanted to visit Paris because of the great art. Many of the greatest artists lived in France and much of their best work is in Paris. My little group of students along with my wife and me had only a week to see and do as much as we could possibly accomplish in a week in Paris. Our days began early in the morning and ended late at night. It was exhilarating and exhausting for me as the leader of the group, as well as for the students.

Some strange events occurred during that week which foreshadowed the climactic event. We were visiting Notre Dame Cathedral, and it was full of tourists. There was a large sign in the entrance written in English stating, "Silence Please." I pointed out the sign to our group and mentioned that it was written in English. The noise inside the cathedral was similar to being in a sports arena during a game. People were yelling at each other across the vast space. Most of the people were speaking English. As we walked around the cathedral it became more disturbing to me that these tourists behaved so horribly. I said to my wife, "I can't stand this anymore. These people have no respect for this church."

Lessons Learned

"What do you care?" she said. "You don't believe in any of this."

"I know but it's not right." I replied.

I was bothered by the disrespect people were showing for this sacred cathedral, and I didn't understand why it bothered me. This continued to frustrate me during the next few days. Why did it upset me that people had no regard for a sacred space? Atheists don't care about such things.

When we visited St. Chappelle cathedral the next day I was so overwhelmed by the beauty of the sacred space I shed a few tears. This had never happened to me in my entire life. The only time I can recall crying in my adult life was when my grandfather died. We had been very close and he treated me like royalty. He died suddenly in his early seventies. I had been raised to believe real men don't cry and crying was a sign of weakness. I never cried because I didn't want to appear weak. Weakness is vulnerability and I strove to be invulnerable. My adolescence had been building a suit of armor around myself to protect myself from emotional hurt. In addition to the iron plated armor of emotional detachment, I had attempted to figure people out so that I could anticipate what they would say and do. I prided myself on being two steps ahead of everyone so that I could anticipate what they were going to say and plan my responses. It didn't always work, but it worked well enough for me to generally know what was happening and be in control. This is living defensively so that you are always prepared offensively. Looking back, it's understandable why this stressful desire to be in control appealed to me considering the abusive childhood that was my home life. It's a disengaged way to live and it robbed me of meaningful interactions and spontaneity in relation to other people and to God.

Another crisis happened when we went to L'Orangerie, which was a separate building of the Louvre museum that held the Impressionist paintings. Claude Monet is one of my favorite artists, and here was a collection of his enormous water lily paintings that he did close to the end of his life. I stood transfixed before these masterpieces. I was actually feeling like I was dissolving into them. The vigorous brush strokes of vibrant colors pulled me into the paintings. It was a dizzying effect. I couldn't move. Without warning I was filled with an irrational and inexplicable fear that if I stayed in front of them any longer I would cease to exist. Feeling totally out of control I ran out of the building to the edge of the Seine River, crying.

My wife came out after me and asked, "What are you doing?"

Lessons Learned

"I think I'm dying," I muttered through my tears.

"What are you talking about?" she asked.

I repeated what I said, and she shook her head in disbelief. Standing there by the edge of the river I tried to regain control of my mind. How can you be so lost in a painting that you imagine you're losing self-awareness? To a person who lived compulsively in self control, this was frightening. It was also embarrassing to do this in front of my students. In a very real sense, I was suffocating in my self-made ego. There is no way to experience the transcendent divine when one is unwilling to let go of the egotistical illusion of control.

How predictable had been my disappointing showdown with God when I was fifteen, based on my determination to be in control! I had gone into Boston on the trolley and gotten off at Copley Square because there was a huge church nearby. This had been my test to find if God was real or not. The church was empty and I'd boldly walked up to the front of the church, standing just below the chancel. I said aloud, "God, if you are real, show me something. Prove you are real." I stood looking at the altar. Nothing happened. Time went by with me standing defiantly watching for a sign. Nothing Happened.

After a short while I walked to the entrance of the church. Turning around and facing the altar I said, "So I knew you

Lessons Learned

are a fake." And I walked out. That incident was my deliberate turning away from God.

But these incidents in Paris indicated something was going on inside me, and I had no idea what was happening. Apparently there was turmoil deep inside that was so disturbing I refused to acknowledge it, but it was being manifested in disturbing emotions that overwhelmed me. This is the danger of trying to be in control of oneself all the time. You have difficulty adjusting to change, and you see change as a threat. These incidents suggest that the divine was speaking to me in ways that I refused to acknowledge because they conflicted with my conscious understanding of who and what I was. I was hostile to God on the level of my rational mind, but there was a deeper part of myself that I rejected that was desperate for a connection to God. It's not easy being an atheist. One has to always keep one's guard up against anything that might affirm God. That defensiveness is the reason atheists are so readily hostile to faith, and most opposed to sincere faith. For the atheist it is hardly worth the effort to combat religion that appears to be irrational or ridiculous. Those kinds of religious expressions only prove to the atheist that religion is delusional. Simple, loving faith in God is a challenge to an atheist's sensibilities because it awakens the conflict within them.

Lessons Learned

We have all come from God the Creator, and everything in the world has come from God. There is nothing apart from God no matter how hard it tries or pretends it is separate from God. God's awareness is total. One way that God can be known to some degree is through observation of the creation. Scientific investigation is the process of looking into that divine plan. Many of the greatest scientists believed in God, scientists such as Isaac Newton and Albert Einstein. On a foundational level there are infinite mysteries behind all observable phenomena which lead one to a belief in something unseen and unknowable. This mysterious force is called God, Creator, Supreme Being, Universal Consciousness, Holy One, Higher Power, and countless other names. Honest intellectual inquiry inevitably leads to the "Source of Being". How often we turn away in fear from the great "I Am". Pride is the enemy of submission to God. Humility grounds us in a relationship with that which is far beyond ourselves. In our society pride is highly valued and rewarded. Humility is associated with weakness and stupidity. Who could admit they are lowly and deficient in our culture? Yet these are precisely the paramount qualities which Christian faith requires. Jesus Christ is the perceived enemy of the egotism of our culture.

We were taught that self-sufficiency is one of the highest virtues. I remember hating to ask anyone for help. To be

Lessons Learned

dependent on anyone was weakness. Asking for help, which included praying, was proof of being deficient. After my conversion, I now ask God for everything and feel completely dependent on God for everything in my life. My deficiencies are glaringly conspicuous to me daily and it is through my dependence upon God that I find wholeness. Before my conversion not only could I not pray to God, it wasn't even possible for me to consider such a thing. When I was dying in the hospital in Paris, suffering pain beyond description, it never occurred to me to pray. People in Alcoholics Anonymous say a person cannot begin the process of recovery until they have reached rock bottom. I relate to that as a former atheist. Atheists are at war with religion, and in the United States of America they are winning the battle. Ultimately, however, they'll lose the war. Will the United States have to hit rock bottom before it turns to God?

As I recount my spiritual journey I have the luxury of hindsight. It's important to share this unpleasant internal struggle to convey why I was given the near-death experience that took me out of this world and into the worlds I refused to believe in. There are reasons why I was given the experience I had, and it's difficult for me to reexamine this ground, but I feel that it's necessary. My hope is that in my testimony, some will find some of their

Lessons Learned

struggles and they will benefit from my exposing the truth of my existence.

On June first 1985 at eleven o'clock in the morning at the Hotel De Lima in Paris, France, there was an explosion in my gut that dropped me to the floor screaming in pain and terror. There had been a slight warning minutes before of what I thought was indigestion, which I'd medicated with some aspirin. My wife called the reception desk of the hotel and the receptionist called an emergency doctor. This doctor arrived in about ten minutes and found me writhing on the floor. He managed to get me onto the bed and examined me. He quickly concluded that I had a perforation of the small stomach and that immediate surgery was required. He explained that this was a life-threatening situation, but that with immediate surgery I would recover in eight weeks. He called an ambulance and then administered what he described as the minimal amount of morphine. He apologized for how little morphine he was giving me, saying that he didn't want to interfere with the anesthetic that I would soon be given for the surgery. Almost immediately I felt partial relief from the acute pain in the core of my abdomen. We felt relieved by his confidence and knowledge, and by his assurance of an immediate remedy to the situation.

Lessons Learned

The two young men who came with the ambulance managed to carry me down the hall and into the elevator. The three of us squeezed into the two-person elevator that carried us from the second to the first floor. They found a chair and carried me down the long flight of stairs to the lobby and into the ambulance. We raced at high speed through the busy streets of Paris across the city to the Cochin public hospital. I was taken to the emergency area and immediately examined by two kind woman doctors. They had me x-rayed and took my medial history. They made it absolutely clear that I would be going straight to surgery and there was no time to waste. An orderly very roughly inserted a tube through my nose and into my stomach. I was placed on a gurney and rushed outside and over several blocks of bumpy pavement to the surgical hospital. We took the elevator up several floors and I was put in a room to await the surgery. I was given no medication and had only the rubber hose down the back of my throat that was supposed to suction out stomach fluids.

The bed had a sheet covering it, and there was no top sheet or pillow. The occupant in the other bed was Monsieur Fluerin. He was a very kind, sixty eight year old man. His wife's father was an American, and we found him to be very sympatric. On the rare occasions when a nurse would enter the room, he would speak to them in

Lessons Learned

French and then translate their comments for us. I did very little talking because the slightest movement aggravated the pain which was getting progressively worse. After about an hour we understood that there was no surgeon available at the hospital and they were in the process of finding one that would do the surgery. I asked my roommate to beg for morphine because what I was given previously had worn off and the pain was unbearable. He was told that only a doctor could prescribe medication, and we would have to wait for the arrival of the doctor, which would be soon.

After several more hours elapsed I was fighting for my life. It was becoming very difficult to breathe. Every breath was causing the digestive fluids in my abdomen to migrate to new areas. What had begun as a specific point of pain had now become a large area of intense agony that was growing bigger all the time. The area of acute pain became my entire torso - from my groin to my shoulders. Breathing was a moment-to-moment challenge. I told Monsieur Fluerin to tell the nurses I was dying, and he did. They said there was nothing they could do until a doctor arrived. I began to realize that I wasn't going to survive. That was terrifying because I knew it meant my annihilation. I kept thinking that this can't be happening to me; I'm thirty-eight years old and too young to die! The thought that troubled me most was why I was

Lessons Learned

conscious when you're supposed to lose consciousness when the pain is overwhelming. Why was I conscious?

There was very little thought going on in my mind. I was in the fetal position and intensely focused on not moving because movement aggravated the pain. The majority of my thoughts were concerned with exhaling and inhaling. It was so painful to breathe that I had to fight the impulse to not breathe with sheer conscious will. If I hadn't done this with what felt like all of my might I would have stopped breathing. This went on for hours. Afterwards, doctors back in the United States told me that my life expectancy under those circumstances was five hours. I was brought to this surgical hospital in Paris around noon and now it was getting dark outside. I was determined to stay alive, but I became so exhausted it was no longer possible to make the effort to breathe as often as I had. I now knew the end was near.

A nurse came into the room at eight thirty and announced that they were unable to locate a doctor and they might have one come on Sunday. I asked my roommate a couple of times to repeat exactly what the nurse had said. After he repeated the nurse's remarks, I called my wife over from the chair she had been sitting in. I told her I was going to die, and it was time to say good bye. I told her I loved her and to tell my children, my parents, my sister, and my friends that I loved them too. My wife wept and

Lessons Learned

said she loved me. She sat down in her chair and wept. I had never seen her weep like that before, and it was horrible to see her so miserable. I closed my eyes, resigned to the cessation of my existence.

Everyone I associated with believed as I did that there was no life beyond death, that humans are biological organisms made up of electro-chemical components that are created in the womb, and all functions end when you die. I knew of no proof of life after death, and conventional science clearly teaches us not to give credence to religious folk tales. We had heard about near-death experiences and dismissed them as natural chemical hallucinations generated by a brain in serious trauma. So we accepted that under certain circumstances the brain released chemicals to create near death experiences to be buffers for the dying process, certainly not indications of consciousness after death.

In the process of dying I experienced something like going to sleep. In fact it was a tremendous relief from the pain I'd undergone for the past nine and a half hours. I was as predisposed to not having a near death experience as anyone could be. I knew that the belief in life after death precedes human history, and that it's a universal feature of almost every religion in the world. I knew that the majority of people in the world believe in life after death, including those who say they are not religious. I believed

Lessons Learned

the evidence had always been anecdotal and unobservable. I was dying just like I'd imagined it would be - complete annihilation.

People have often asked me if I died, and I believe I did. There was no doctor or nurse present, so no one checked my vital signs. My wife was consumed by grief, knowing that I was dying. There is no scientific proof that I physically died, and whether I was clinically dead isn't important. What is certain is that my experience, to which I'm a reliable witness, did not happen while I, my consciousness, was in my body. There are millions of persons all over the world who have reported near-death experiences with similarities to my experience, and I find commonality with them. Non-experiencers choose one of three possibilities – all near death experiences are lies, lunacy, or the truth. What happened to me next is the truth to the best of my ability to state it.

Much of the experience is ineffable and it's frustrating to try to communicate it. The most important part of the experience was experiencing the love of Jesus. If I could put into words and successfully convey the love that Jesus has for me and for all of us, it would change the world.

As a parallel – if I could find the words to express the horrors of hell that I experienced, it would make an indelible impression. I tell only part of that story. If I

Lessons Learned

wrote everything that happened to me, and all the things Jesus told me, I would fill volumes. It's beyond my objective in this little testimony to go into the depth of all that I was given. The following is therefore only a brief sketch of my near death experience.

Lessons Learned

1. Even when we refuse to acknowledge God, there is still some appreciation for the sacred in us. The innermost center of every person desires to be loved, have a relationship with, and win approval from God, Our Creator, whether we know or are completely ignorant of Him.
2. Many times it takes an extreme crisis for a person to let go of their ego sufficiently to call upon God. Suffering can sometimes be the motivation for tremendous spiritual growth.
3. Near death experiences can be the opportunity for an awakening to God, love, and some understanding of life after death. Every NDE is unique and for that individual, although there are many strong similarities in NDE's.
4. There are only two possibilities when we die and leave this world. We are either going toward God in heaven drawn by our love, hope, and faith, or we are repelled by God and we will find ourselves in a world devoid of God and all His goodness.
5. God gave me this experience of heaven and hell so that I might re-examine my life and follow Jesus Christ. By living a life devoted to Jesus I am obligated to acknowledge Him in the hope others will find the love and peace He gives.

Chapter 5 – The Greeting Committee

When I awoke from unconsciousness I was standing next to the bed. Happily the pain that had engulfed me was gone, and something new was happening to me. I found my sight, hearing, smell, touch, and taste to be heightened beyond anything I had experienced before. I tested my senses and was amazed at how much more alive I felt. There was a body in the bed that I'd occupied and its head was turned away from me. I bent over to look at the face. Impossibly it resembled me down to the last detail. This was impossible because I was looking at something that was the mirror image of me, but it seemed it wasn't alive. I rejected it as an impostor. How and why it was there was beyond comprehension. I felt more alive than I'd ever felt in my life. I was not that corpse-thing lying in the bed!

I was very confused and tried to talk to my wife who was on the opposite side of the bed. There was no response. She just wept with her head facing downward. It was very upsetting to me when she seemed to totally ignore me. I gave up, turned to my roommate and yelled in his face. He stared through me as if I wasn't there. This added to my confusion. The very plainly furnished room was

Lessons Learned

brightly lit and it was uncomfortable being there with a dead imposter in my bed and two people who refused to acknowledge my existence.

I heard people calling me by my name from the hallway beyond the room. I moved to the doorway and could barely see a number of figures standing away from the light of the room in the shadowy hall. They were insisting that I go with them. I asked if they had come from the doctor to take me to surgery. Instead of answering directly, they said they knew all about me and had been waiting a long time, and it was time for me to go with them. I could only assume they were taking me to the operating room. When I stepped out of the room light into the shadows I had a bad feeling about following these strangers, but I felt there was no other choice.

We walked and walked. There were no features to this realm we were in; it just became gradually darker and darker. Soon they had encircled me and were leading me onward. I'd ask questions and they would become increasingly annoyed and evasive. I stopped doing that because it made them angry. By this time I was afraid but didn't know where I could go to get away from them. I was lost. The darkness had become utter blackness and I couldn't see anything. I refused to go farther with them, and they began to push and pull at me.

Lessons Learned

I resisted and fought back with all my might. It was hopeless because the group had grown into a huge mob of people, all wanting to get a piece of the action - which was all about tormenting me. The pain was worse than what one would experience in this world because my senses were greatly heightened. They were biting, tearing, probing, and degrading me. It is too disgusting and painful for me to describe more explicitly. They wanted to cause as much pain as possible. These people had lived in the world that I'd lived in. They had rejected God, and God had allowed them what they desired, to be apart from God. The consequence of that choice, which they'd freely made, was separation from God. That separation included separation from all that we enjoy in our lives – namely, the gifts of God. God gives light, and they live in darkness. God gives the beauty of the creation, and they live in a world devoid of everything but themselves. God gives love, hope, and faith, and they live in hate, despair, and unbelief. Their misery is beyond words. I don't know what will happen to them.

Some speculate that they'll stay in this state for time-without-end. Others believe they will devolve into annihilation. Still others believe that God will find a way to redeem them. There are Biblical texts that can support all these theories. What I do know is that they've chosen this fate by their rejection of God. Furthermore, I know it's not

Lessons Learned

God's desire that anyone would suffer this fate, but God is just and everyone reaps what they sow. God has done everything lovingly possible so that humans would not suffer the consequences of their actions. God has put a plan into motion that allows for free will in order to make possible a choice to receive God's mercy and forgiveness for our sin. God's salvation is the life, death, and resurrection of Jesus Christ. Why do people choose to reject it? I look back at my life and wish I could have confronted my younger, foolish self and told it the truth. But God has given me the gift of experiencing the horror of hell so that I might testify to its existence. Most people don't believe there is a hell, and they are certain they would never go to such a place. This is the biggest deception going on in the world today.

I suspect that most of the people in hell thought they were good people by their own standards of what is good. No one is good by the standard of a Holy God. Everyone desperately needs the forgiveness of Jesus Christ, which is freely given. Why are people afraid to receive the love of God? Why are so many people hostile to Jesus? The people in hell that I met there hated God, and they hated Jesus. Now they fight for dominance just as they did in the world, and their war for supremacy never ends. I am not an authority on the subject of hell because I experienced only a small portion of the vast world of separation from

Lessons Learned

God. It's also true that what I experienced is only that portion that God gave me the opportunity to be a part of. It most definitely gets much worse. The real torment of hell is not the physical pain which is inflicted. The real torment of hell is the emotional agony of hopelessness. Many cultures and religions teach about hell. Jesus spoke about hell often. I suspect that people are ignorant of the reality of hell because they choose to be.

My spirit recognized the spirit of the people who attacked me and I know them as they knew me. It is my hope and desire that no one will go to that place, but there is no way I can stop them if that is what they choose. Everyone gets exactly what they deserved by the life they led. God knows our every thought, word, and deed. God judges by what is in the heart while we judge by appearances. God's wisdom is perfect and God's judgment is absolute. I know that God desires no one to go to hell, but God will give each person what is in their heart. God is not deceived by our pretense.

They left me torn apart on the ground of that place of abject darkness. The physical pain I was consumed by was not as great as the emotional pain I was feeling. Lying there ripped apart, I heard a voice say, "Pray to God!" Three times this voice spoke to me. I rejected the idea of prayer at first because I did not pray, and I didn't know how to pray. After the third time of being instructed to

Lessons Learned

pray, I tried to remember things I had been taught as a child. I thought prayer was something you recited from memory and I tried to recall anything I had memorized as a child. In my frustration with the difficulty of trying to recall something appropriate I began to mutter some phrases that included the mention of God. That got a powerful reaction from the people around me.

These people became extremely agitated and they responded by screaming: There is no God! – We're going to really hurt you now if you don't stop! – No one can hear you! These were accompanied by a torrent of obscenities. It was clear that they either hated or denied the existence of God. Despite their threats they retreated away from me. Praying to God repelled them. This encouraged me to pray harder and louder. They continued yelling but kept backing away into the gloom. I shouted anything I could think of that had God connected to it. Curiously, the sword of truth, as the word of God is called, is powerful even in the hands of a sinner. The prayers drove them far enough away that I could no longer hear them. Alone, I lay there in my wretched state thinking about what had happened to me. Without any theological training the best I could determine was what I could fathom in very worldly terms. I concluded that I had simply lived a rotten life and this had resulted in being flushed down the sewer into the cesspool of being. I

Lessons Learned

didn't think of it as punishment; rather it seemed like justice. I was convinced I deserved this fate and that the people I'd encountered deserved their fates and were filled with the same self-loathing I felt. As I thought about my life and interactions with others I felt I'd been a failure at everything. My responsibilities as a son, brother, husband, father, teacher, and neighbor had all failed. I could have done so much better and wouldn't have deserved the cesspool. Worse, the cesspool isn't temporary. If you haven't experienced eternity you can't possibly comprehend it. In eternity, there is a present that has no limit. In our world the present is so fleeting it's difficult to fully experience it. We invest most of our consciousness in the past and future, and both are as fleeting as our thoughts. In eternal time there's only the present, and it's infinite. Can you even begin to imagine what it means to be lost in eternity? A second is a century and a minute is an eon. There is no time as we know it in eternity. I had eternity to think about my life, and I was in despair over what I'd discovered. Who could save me from this damnation?

My subconscious mind searched through my life and found a boy sitting in a Sunday school classroom singing "Jesus Loves Me". I remembered being that child and believing those words as perhaps only a child can. I wanted that faith in Jesus again. I started to doubt again,

Lessons Learned

but rejected my doubts and in desperation stood on the faith of a child. I shouted into the darkness, "Jesus please save me!", and I meant it. I know, now, that that was the single most important decision of my life. Now, I pray that everyone will shout those words and mean it.

Almost immediately after shouting those words, in the total darkness a tiny light appeared overhead. It became brighter and appeared to be getting closer, faster, and faster. At first I thought the light would burn and consume me because it was brighter than the sun and moving directly upon me. Instead of being engulfed in scorching flames I felt love. Hands and arms emerged from this radiance and they reached down and touched me. Very quickly all the gore and brokenness was restored to wholeness. That was amazing enough, but what was far more significant was the feeling of love that filled me. There are no adequate words to describe this love. I knew this was Jesus. He loves me. Jesus really loves me. There are no words to speak this love, but you can have it if you want it. But you have to ask for it and be ready to receive this awesome love. Only Jesus can give it to you, and he wants to give it to you! Jesus loves us far more than we know. Here I was a piece of filth on the fringe of hell and Jesus answered my prayer. He will answer your prayer if you want Him.

Lessons Learned

Meeting Jesus was the turning point in my life. Everything has changed since then. I consider that moment to be the time I was born to real life. I was filled with the Spirit of Jesus. From that time on and in the decades since, that is all I really want. Sometimes I feel it like that again, and other times not. I know that the next time I leave this world I will be totally with and in Jesus Christ. I can hardly wait for that day! I often think, "Oh, God be patient with me because I want to be with Jesus and all the saints!" I try to do the best with the time I've been given and not be too homesick for my heavenly home.

Jesus put His arms around me and carried me up and out of that world of darkness. I held onto to Him and cried like a baby. It was as though I had been dead and then was alive. I was lost and then was found. As Jesus sped toward a world of light with me, I intensely felt the contrast and thought about what a filthy rag I had been. That feeling was so profound that I thought Jesus had made a mistake and I didn't belong in heaven. The moment I had that thought we immediately stopped, still far from heaven, and Jesus spoke to me, with his voice in my mind, saying, "We don't make mistakes. You do belong here."

I have been asked many times why Jesus rescued me from hell. I have several responses to that question. Jesus knows everything and He knew I was going to call on Him. He knew all about me before I was born. He was there

72

Lessons Learned

when I was baptized as a boy. He let me go astray and He was waiting for me to pray to Him. He knew I would return to this world and tell everyone about His love. Two thousand years ago He told what could have been my story in the parable of the prodigal son. I am the prodigal son. God knows what needs to be done. God is in control. When I called out to Jesus, that was precisely what He had been patiently waiting for, for many years. In four different places the Bible says, "Anyone who calls upon the name of the Lord shall be saved." Another reason that I feel God rescued me is that an entire convent, led by Sister Dolores, was praying for me daily for many years. Prayer is powerful. Results of prayer aren't always immediate, but prayer can do things that can't be done any other way. God does not make mistakes. God has a good purpose for our lives if we love God. Now I was going to learn my purpose for being born at the tender age of thirty eight.

Being a Christian is to know Jesus and to follow Him. The church is His instrument to help us do that. There have been times when churches go astray because people lose sight of Jesus. If the church didn't exist, would there be any knowledge of Jesus in the world? I lost sight of Jesus because He wasn't the focal point of my church. I have to remind myself of that all the time. For a myriad of reasons

Lessons Learned

it's easy to lose sight of Jesus as the focal point of the church.

Jesus and I began to converse by His knowing my every thought and by His voice speaking in my mind. He told me He knew everything I had ever thought. He said he had friends that He wanted me to meet and He called out to them in musical tones that seemed like chimes. A group of beings bathed in brilliant radiance came to us, and they formed a circle around us. I now call these beings, angels. They had a record of my life and wanted to show it to me. At first I was delighted to have this much attention. The episodes of my life review began with my birth and proceeded chronologically. Everything was happiness in my family in the beginning, but as the years passed, dysfunction entered the dynamics of the family and destroyed the happiness. It was hard watching the family come apart, and to see abusive behavior destroying love and trust. I saw myself withdrawing emotionally from everyone to avoid being hurt. Jesus and the angels shared their joy and their sadness as we watched these scenes. We could also feel what others in my life were feeling and even hear their thoughts. It was so sad to see how we hurt each other. There is a common saying "Jesus loves the sinner, but hates the sin." This is precisely what I learned from Jesus. During the life review, I became very

Lessons Learned

ashamed of my behavior in the family – which may best be described as emotional withdrawal.

Jesus and the angels rejoiced when I was compassionate and shared their disapproval with me over the times I was selfish. Unfortunately, as I aged my egotism outweighed my compassion. It became so painful to watch that I begged Jesus to stop the life review. He told me it was necessary to see all of it. To my surprise, what I thought were triumphs of my life were unimportant to them. The acts of compassion were the only things they cared about. I had missed the whole purpose of being alive. God made me for a reason, and I never knew what that was. I learned that we are here to love one another. Jesus taught that repeatedly in the Bible. It is strange how we can miss that lesson. The Bible records that when Jesus was asked what the greatest teaching is, he responded, "Love God with all of your heart, mind and soul, and love your neighbor as yourself." His last commandment was, "Love one another." This is the standard by which we either experience the afterlife as heaven or hell.

Jesus asked me if I had any questions. I said I have a million questions and I asked everything I could think to ask. He answered all my questions patiently and simply. He is the best teacher I've ever had. He used many audio-visual aids. During our conversation I couldn't tell if we traveled through time and space or whether he created

Lessons Learned

the reality around us. There are many things that I've never discussed because it hasn't seemed prudent. Some things Jesus told me are controversial by some peoples' opinions so I avoid those topics to stay centered on Jesus and not create controversy.

This question and answer period was a more extensive learning experience than my three years of graduate school. I've relied on these lessons ever since and they have always served me well. I later had the privilege of going to an excellent seminary for three years and was well prepared for that graduate education because of my time with Jesus. After this experience I became enamored of the Bible because so much of what He told me I came to find in the Bible. When I searched other religions I didn't always find the same correspondence with the truths Jesus taught me. I will cover some of the questions and answers in later chapters.

I learned that when we die we go to another world. The physical laws of this world are not applicable in the next world which, one could say, operates on a very different physics. We're not alone when we die and we'll be met by beings that are attracted to us by the qualities of our hearts and souls. We are either attracted to the world of light or the world of darkness, and there is no in-between place. Jesus said, "And if I go and prepare a place for you, I will come again and take you to myself, so that where I

Lessons Learned

am, there you may be also." To my knowledge, no one has ever made a statement comparable to this promise from Jesus. Jesus is trustworthy and his statement is true. So by faith in Jesus – by my awareness of and desire to be with Jesus – I will be met by Him and taken to heaven, to a place he prepared for me long ago.

Without Jesus, one can expect a greeting committee of people who will deceive you and they will take you to a place to which you would never want to go. If you knew how horrible that place is you wouldn't want anyone to go there, not even your worst enemy. But many people do go there and it's because they have refused God's invitation to receive a rescue from sin and death through His Son Jesus Christ.

We could go off on numerous tangents by asking about this or that possibility. We can speculate and theorize all kinds of scenarios all of our lives. These speculations do not change the simple fact that we are either going toward God or away from God. There is no neutral position. To be neutral or to be apathetic – these are subtle forms of hatred. God has made the way, the truth, and the life clear for all to know. God has lived the way, the truth, and the life to teach us the way home so that we may decide which way to go. My hope is that all of us will chose to put our faith in Jesus.

Lessons Learned

Lessons Learned

1. When our body dies, our consciousness continues and we carry all of our experiences, thoughts, and feelings with us. Dying and leaving this world is very confusing and there are beings waiting for us when we die. We are either welcomed by God's agents to bring us to heaven or we are taken by those who have rejected God and we are taken into darkness.
2. Both heaven and hell are very complex and have many levels. In heaven, as one grows in their Christ nature, they ascend toward God. In hell, people increase in depravity and torment as they descent into the abyss.
3. The people in hell chose that fate by their decisions in life which essentially rejected God or what God represents. They are reaping what they sowed.
4. The Bible states, "Anyone who calls upon the name of the Lord shall be saved." Even in one's dying process, Jesus saves.
5. Meeting Jesus is the greatest experience of my life, and it completely changed my life. Jesus has helped me ever since I became the person I was created to be from the beginning. Everyone needs to know Jesus.

Lessons Learned

Chapter 6 – Going Home

After Jesus answered all of my questions there was only one thing left for me to do, and that was to ask Him to take me to heaven. I had asked many questions about heaven, and He had told me and showed me many things about it. You would think everyone would want to go to heaven, and considering the alternative, it is the better choice. Heaven is full of wonders, free of suffering, and completely ruled by the love of God. It's not possible to say enough good things about heaven. It's unfortunate that some propagate simplistic and silly views of heaven, because it is the most interesting and varied place in the universe. After Jesus showed me some parts of heaven I was ready to go there forever.

That was when Jesus told me I was going back to the world, and I was not going to heaven at this time. I could not accept this terrible disappointment. I had developed an intimacy with Jesus which goes beyond friendship and had no reservation about expressing myself openly to Him. I had presumed I was sufficiently prepared to go to the joys and wonders of heaven. Jesus patiently explained that I was not ready to go to heaven, and I would not be compatible there. He explained that it was necessary for me to live the way He had explained to me so that one day I would come to heaven and have developed the

Lessons Learned

qualities of character required in the heavenly realm. When He said this I knew He was right about His assessment of my character, but I was desperate to go to heaven regardless of my shortcomings.

Heaven is an extremely complex world, much more so than the world we know. It is totally under the rule and love of God. Nothing incompatible with God can reside in heaven. Saying with your lips you want to go to heaven, or that you love Jesus – these are not the only qualifications one needs to enter heaven. To enter into heaven a person has to fully intend to love God with all of their heart, mind, and soul, and to love their neighbor as themselves. This cannot be faked. God knows a person's heart. No one is going to enter heaven opposed to God. When we go to heaven we are not perfect, but we must have the desire to be perfect before God. Jesus will help us achieve perfection. Our entire lives are a process of sanctification, and that process is completed in heaven. The qualification is to have that desire to please God and love God in the center of our being. Without that desire we cannot enter heaven at any level. By God's grace we will become like Christ in our heavenly progress toward God.

I informed Jesus that the world was a cruel place – full of evil and ugliness. How could He send me to such a terrible world? He acknowledged the cruelty, evil, and ugliness in the world. Then He said there is also much love,

Lessons Learned

goodness, and beauty in the world. Before He could continue I challenged Him by repeating my question, "How could you send me back there?"

Jesus made it clear that what is in one's heart is what would attract – that if you seek cruelty you will find cruelty, but if you are loving you will find love; if you seek evil, you will find that, but if you are good in your heart you will find goodness; if you seek ugliness, you will also find that, but if you seek beauty, you will see beauty everywhere. It was not possible to dispute what he said. I have since found what he told me to be profoundly true. This by no means suggests we create reality. It does mean our perception of the world around us is determined by the state of our inner being, our heart. We project our inner selves onto the experience of the world. The perception of light is by its contrast with dark. We come to discern good from evil by experiencing both. God gives us the mind, heart and soul to make those distinctions and to know the difference. This is why we have been given this life experience to determine what we will choose. The choice comes down to choosing God or not. When one chooses God it becomes a passionate pursuit. If you do not feel passionate about the love of God you are far from God and need to make radical changes in your life. God is not pleased by tepid feelings toward our Creator. To receive the love of God and to reciprocate

Lessons Learned

that love is why we are created. There is no indifference in love. My hope is to please God by my intention to love God in everything that I do. The results of my works are secondary to my intentions. I cannot control the response to my love which may be rejected. We are only responsible to love, according to our ability to love.

I asked Jesus what I would do if I went back to the world, and before He could answer, I'd already considered going back to the world and building a shrine to Jesus. Because I was an artist I began to imagine a huge construction that would be a masterpiece of stained glass and modern architecture that people from all over the world would come to see. Jesus laughed as he observed the grandiose visual images racing through my imagination.

Paraphrasing His reply, He said, 'We do not need another shrine. Men build these things because they think they glorify us, but we have little use for them. People build them for themselves. You are not going back to hide yourself away in some monumental project and neglecting those around you. You were created to change the world, and that is what you are to do when you go back.'

This was a shock to me; Jesus had no use for my shrine. I understood about hiding from relationships by becoming obsessed with a big project. God was not particularly

Lessons Learned

impressed with monuments to glorify God. The statement Jesus made about changing the world was also disturbing. I responded by making it clear to Him that I was not going to change the world because I didn't know how. To further convince Him, I pointed out that there were those who wanted to change the world, and they turned out to do more harm than good, like Hitler, Stalin, Mao Tse Tung, and other tyrants. Jesus was slightly amused by my total misunderstanding of what He wanted me to do in the world.

He said that I was to go back and love the person I am with, and that will change the world.

Now it was my turn to scoff at His suggestion. How could you change the world by loving the person you are with? I told Him that the world doesn't want to change, and loving someone is not going to change the course of the world.

He said that this is God's plan to change the world; that when one person loves another person, it changes the world.

I informed Him that this was too simple, and it would never work.

Jesus answered that this is God's will, and it will work because God has made it such that one person will love

Lessons Learned

another and that that person will carry that love, and love another until the world is filled with love; that the world will be changed by love from one to another.

My response was to ask about a situation where the person who is loved gets run over by a truck, making the whole plan fall apart. I asked Him how I could love enough people.

In response, He asked me if I thought I were the only one in God's plan for the world. He said there are millions of people changing the world and millions more becoming part of the plan, that all of God's angels are making the plan happen, and that I will be one small but important part of God's plan. He added that this is the will of God and it is happening now, and that I have the opportunity to participate in God's will for the world, and that it is my choice.

I agreed that it may be possible for me to love the person I was with, but I had no idea how hard it is to be truly loving. When you are with a loving person, it is easy to love in return; but how often is that the situation? Frequently we are with people who are not especially loving and they are much more difficult to love. They have their own motives and desires, which can be quite distracting from love. The people who are angry and hateful are the most difficult to love. How challenging it is

Lessons Learned

to not be caught up in their emotions and join them in their passions for conflict. For several decades I have attempted to be a more loving person, and yet there is so much more for me to learn about love! To be intentionally a part of God's plan is a choice that each person has to decide to make. One has to work at it every day in every new situation. It can never be taken for granted. Just when you think you have achieved a certain ability to love people, a situation arises that makes you realize how little you are able to respond with genuine love. The nuances of love are very subtle, and old formulas become obsolete and hypocritical. Love is the lesson that never ends.

When I started to read the Bible it became apparent that love was the subject of the books in the Bible. Jesus made it perfectly clear in His commandments to His disciples, when He said, "Love one another." This was His great commandment to them and to us. When I read this in the Bible I knew the Bible truly held the word of God. It is shocking how this great teaching gets obscured and even lost in the Christian churches. Since the commandment to love is the foundational teaching of God, everything must be weighed against it. Without love we are nothing. We are just "a noisy gong or clanging cymbal." Saint Paul said it so well in his letter to the Corinthians.

Lessons Learned

I told Jesus He could not send me back to the world because it would break my heart. He was my best friend, and I had never been loved as He loved me. If He sent me to the world I could not live without Him. Before I knew Him, I never saw Him or heard Him. Would it be like that if He made me come back to the world?

Jesus told me that I will not see Him or hear Him in the world, but that He has made it known to me that He was always with me and will always be with me. So I responded to Him with what was my deepest concern. I explained to Jesus I had never been loved as intensely as He loved me and I had never been known as fully as He knew me. It would break my heart to not see Him or hear Him in the world, and I knew I could not live without Him in my life. He could not send me back to the world because I would forget His love and that would kill me. Jesus understood the depths of my despair at the thought of being separated from Him, even though He assured me He would be present to me in spite my inability to see Him. He told me that if I prayed, I would know he was with me at times and I would feel His love.

I asked Him how I could pray so that I could feel His presence and love.

He instructed me to go to a quiet place and tell Him everything that is going on in my life – to be completely

Lessons Learned

honest, and just let everything come out in the open. He said that when it is necessary, He will allow me to feel His presence and that will give me the feeling of love that I seek.

I told Him this would be the only way that I could go back to the world.

My hope to go to heaven was crushed by my desire to trust and please Jesus by returning to the world. It was inevitable I was going to concede to His superior understanding of things and I would return to the world. From what He showed me, heaven is so much better than the world in every way, and by comparison, no one would want to be in the world. I know our lives are brief and heaven is eternal, so it is a relatively short time in the world, but the world can be very difficult. It is absolutely necessary that we live in this world and learn the lessons here so that we will be able to make the choice to be obedient to God's will or not. But there is no short cut to heaven.

I told Jesus I would go back, and immediately I was back. The horrendous pain I had experienced before I left was back. I gasped for air, struggling to breathe. The nurse who had come to the room earlier, returned to the room, and she announced that a doctor had arrived at the hospital and I would be having the surgery soon. Two

Lessons Learned

attendants grabbed my wife and escorted her out of the room. The nurse and the orderlies proceeded to prepare me for surgery. They dry-shaved the hair from my torso.

As I was wheeled past my wife on the way to the elevator, I said, "Everything is going to be good now!" She tried to smile back as I went by her. I was confident the surgery would be successful and I would be returning to the United States in a month or two. Somehow I was guaranteed a successful outcome because Jesus was with me and I was going to have a new life. I had been lost and now was found. I had died and been reborn. I was aware that I was a new person and the old self was gone. It felt as if I had just been born anew and this was the first day of my life. My old self was just some baggage that I would have to deal with when it interfered with my new self.

I had asked Jesus if I would suffer if I came back to the world, and he had told me I would. He kept to his word on that matter. But, pain had a different effect on me when I returned. I refused to let it control me. I would not let pain capture my full attention. I would talk to it and compartmentalize it. I would no longer let pain master me. I would learn how to master pain. This doesn't mean I could always vanquish the sensations. There were times when I could pray pain away. When I could not make it go away, I could make it diminish enough so that I could still think and have a life in spite of it. I would never allow pain

Lessons Learned

to overwhelm me again. Jesus was a tremendous resource of accomplishing my victory over pain. Trust in the presence of Jesus is far better than any narcotic! If only all people knew about the "Great Physician!" Pain is a function of the mind, and we can have control of the way the sensation of pain controls us. With the help of God we can even eliminate pain from our consciousness.

When I awoke from surgery the first time the nurses were washing my abdomen. The soapy water was warm and the rinse water was cold. They kept repeating applications of the warm and cold water, rubbing gently around the incision which ran from my chest to my groin. There were fifty-six staples holding the puckered skin together. I opened my eyes and smiled at the nurse. She screamed. She ran across the room to the doctor and told him that I was awake! He told her that was not possible and came across the room to inspect me. I was tired and didn't want to talk to the doctor so I closed my eyes and pretended to be asleep. After he left I peeked at the nurse and she smiled back at me. The next time I awoke I began to think about my time with Jesus. I was in a terrible dilemma because it was now imperative that I change my life; but what, I wondered would I change.

I had invested everything I knew into becoming who I was at the age of thirty-eight, and now I had to tear it all apart and start rebuilding everything. This was not a pleasant

Lessons Learned

prospect. The other problem was my concern for my wife, my children, my family, and my friends. Since they were all heathens like me, their fate was probably not heaven either. No one should go to hell; it is more terrible than anyone can imagine. God doesn't want anyone to go to hell, but many people are going there because they have rejected God. What could I say to them to convince them they must change their lives? I wanted everyone to know Jesus because He is the most loving, wonderful, and kind friend. I had to find a way to convince them of the urgency of receiving Jesus in their hearts. But, I wondered, how do you do this?

I thought if I concentrated on love, they would be drawn to the love Jesus and only Jesus can give. I knew that they would resist a hard sell to Christianity. My background as a hard core atheist informed me of the hostility to Christianity that I was facing in presenting Jesus as Savior. Little did I know at that time I was to lose almost everybody because I loved Jesus. I was so filled with the love of Jesus Christ that I naively thought it would be irresistible to those who had that same emptiness in their hearts.

Sunday afternoon my wife came into the room to see me for the first time. I told her, "It's all love!"

"I love you," She said.

Lessons Learned

"I know you love me, but it's all love," I responded.

"Your friends love you," she answered.

"I know that, but it's all love. It is a big, huge ocean of love," I insisted.

"What are you talking about?" She asked. "Maybe you need to sleep more."

At that moment it dawned on me that this was not going to be easy to help anyone know Jesus and His Love. I cried, and my wife left the room. How do you tell anyone about the love of Jesus? If you could get them to experience it they would know. But how many people are even willing to ask Him? I am not interested in getting people to join my personal religion or a cult. I only want them to know the amazing grace of God that Jesus gives. I appreciate why many people are skeptical of religious organizations. I love my church, but that is not what is required of people! They must love God and that is the way, the truth, and the life of Christ. The rest of my life has been trying to find ways to present Jesus so that people will seek Him and want Him to live in them. To taste His Spirit is to crave more and more.

Lessons Learned

Lessons Learned

1. Heaven is for people who have done their best to know God, love God, and follow God's commandments as revealed in the person of Jesus. We are all sinners, and Jesus Christ has made it possible for us to go to heaven and become perfected.
2. We are given this life to develop our whole self to seek God or to reject God. Everything we think and do is based in our relationship to God and will determine our fate after this life.
3. We can know and experience God through Jesus Christ in this world. Jesus teaches us intimacy with God by loving God and one another. By living a life pleasing to God we grow in our closeness to God.
4. God has a plan to transform this world and each of us has an important part in that plan. We are to give ourselves to Jesus Christ and follow his example to the best of our ability.
5. After our conversion, we find it difficult to explain ourselves to those who have never experienced God.

Chapter 7 – Reconstruction

Tuesday they returned me to the room I originally occupied when I was first brought to this hospital. My roommate was away from the room and I lay alone in the bed. An audible voice said, "You will not get well here. You must go home on Monday." I looked around the room and there was no one there.

"I don't believe this," I shouted back to the empty room.

"Believe," came back the reply.

What was I to do? Part of me thought hearing voices was a sure sign of insanity. Part of me thought God was speaking to me and my life depended on believing what I heard. I thought about it and concluded that it was better to trust the voice than to disobey.

When my wife came that afternoon to visit me, I told her to buy plane tickets for Monday to take us home to Kentucky. To my surprise she said she would get the tickets. This was completely uncharacteristic of her. She was an attorney and did not take orders from me. This demand was contrary to our understanding that I needed many weeks of recuperation before we could travel. I was also aware we had no money to buy the tickets. She left the room immediately and returned a few minutes later.

Lessons Learned

She reported she had gone to a pay phone and called her parents in Iowa to send her money to buy the tickets. They told her they would call her back. In minutes they called her back. They told her they had called their bank in Iowa and talked to a manager who had just returned from Paris. He had had an emergency in Paris and had required money sent from the Iowa bank to Paris and knew how to get it done. My wife's father told her to go to a certain bank and the amount of two thousand dollars would be waiting for her. She said to me that she was going to get the money and the plane tickets and would be back soon.

An hour later she returned to the room with two one way tickets to Kentucky for Monday morning. "Why did you do that?" I asked.

"You told me to," she responded.

"But I don't know if we will be able to use them," I retorted.

"Do you want me to return the tickets?" she asked.

"No," I said. "I think we will need them."

We didn't talk about the tickets anymore because I didn't know what to say about them. I was very weak, metal staples ran down my chest and abdomen, and several drainage tubes came out of my body. She left the room and I began again to think about the tickets. Aloud, I said

Lessons Learned

something like, 'I don't know what is going on! It's not nice of you to have us buy tickets that we won't be able to use. How am I going to get well enough to fly home in a few days?'

"Believe," was the audible reply, in a loud and clear voice.

So I resigned, then and there, to the fact we would fly home on Monday. During the next days I got sicker and weaker. After a couple of days they stopped giving me pills. I was concerned because I was deteriorating and there was no further treatment. On Friday a nurse removed every other staple. On Saturday the nurse returned and removed the remaining staples. The large wound looked red and swollen. I was convinced I would be in no condition to leave the hospital. Again I spoke to the empty room, saying something like, 'I know I'm supposed to believe, but this isn't going to happen.' I paused, and continued, 'I know, I know, but it's really hard to believe.'

On Sunday morning, when I awoke something was different. I felt well. So I got up and went into the tiny bathroom connected to the room and proceeded to wash. I shampooed my hair, washed my body from head to toes, brushed my teeth, and shaved. This was all done from a small sink because there was no bathtub or shower. I felt like a new man because I had not bathed in a week. My

Lessons Learned

wife had brought clothes for me to wear on Friday, so for the first time I dressed in normal clothes. When my wife arrived in the afternoon I told her it was time to go.

We were walking down the hall of the hospital when a nurse caught us and started yelling at us. She was insistent we were not leaving. She immediately got a doctor to confront us. He informed us we could not leave because I had not been discharged. I informed him he was mistaken and I was discharged (which was not true). He went away and returned a few minutes later and apologized and said I was discharged and we were free to go. We took a taxi to the hotel and I went to bed to rest because we had to get up very early for our eight-thirty flight home. My wife had purchased business class tickets because she knew I would need to recline on the long flight. I crossed the Atlantic Ocean covered in five blankets trying to sleep. I know the people around us were very uncomfortable being in close proximity to me because they were afraid of catching whatever I had that made me look so sick.

In New York we had a four-hour layover before our flight to Kentucky and I was resting in a wheelchair. I was getting very weak and became concerned that I wouldn't be able to get on the plane home. I wheeled myself into the men's restroom and prayed to God to give me the strength to make it home. My prayer was answered and

Lessons Learned

we arrived in Kentucky at night. We went home because I was too exhausted to face going to the hospital. Early the next morning we went to the hospital and were met by our family doctor. He examined me and was clearly concerned about my condition. He told me I had severe pneumonia, collapsed lungs, acute peritonitis, and liver failure. "I don't know how you made it here!" he exclaimed.

"I have friends," I replied. I really wanted to tell him about Jesus and the angels, but was too tired to talk. I was also concerned he would think I was crazy if I told him what had happened. I decided I would tell him latter when I was stronger. A few days later I told him a little about what had happened, and he did have trouble believing me.

I was put on the critical list and kept in isolation. Everyone who visited me had to wear a gown and a mask. There were numerous doctors visiting me every day. The problem was that the infection in my abdomen was spreading and my belly looked like I was nine months pregnant. I couldn't eat or drink. I was very weak. My eyesight began to fail. It was impossible for me to follow conversations. I would be trying to comprehend the first few words of a sentence spoken to me and the person was already into the next sentence. Everyone told me I was doing fine and not to worry. I was so weak I couldn't

Lessons Learned

lift my head from the pillow. I had intravenous lines in both hands and all kinds of bags of fluids hanging next to me. This went on for weeks. I would later find out that my condition was so critical during that time that my wife was told they did not know whether I would live another day, and to anticipate my death.

Living on the edge of life and death was not troublesome to me. There was a strong desire to die so that I could return to Jesus and be taken to heaven. I was well aware that I must not attempt to cause my death because this would be a terrible rejection of the gift of life that I had been given. Suicide would be displeasing to God. I was depressed by my ever-decreasing abilities. I had been in the same bed for weeks. I was losing my capacity to see and understand conversation. The most critical concern I had was the scorn that I received from everyone when I tried to tell them about Jesus and the angels. I did not want to speak about the terrors of hell because that was far too painful for me to speak about. I have never spoken about what really goes on in hell because it is beyond grotesque. The desire to testify to the love of Jesus consumed me, and the desire to share that knowledge never has diminished. I tried to hug and kiss everyone who came into the room. That was rebuffed, because no one wants to touch a very sick person. I tried to understand that, but I wanted to share the love of Jesus in

Lessons Learned

that simple gesture. I could sense the rejection of my speaking about Jesus. Years later I learned from two nurses who had attended me that I was a common joke in the hospital. People would come to visit me just to hear the ridiculous experience of this dying man talking about the love of Jesus and the angels.

The angels would appear to me daily, but only when I was alone. They never appeared if I had company so that I could never get verification of their visits. They came to encourage me to continue to live and assure me that they were always with me. They were so beautiful and kind, I begged them to take me home – which is heaven were we truly belong. They reminded me of my duty to care for my wife and a child, which is something Jesus had also told me during my time with him. They told me that I would get better in time. They reminded me to trust in God. Mostly they just loved me and helped me persevere in my dire condition. Whenever they left I wanted to talk about them and describe them to the next person who entered the room. These descriptions of the angels were met with ridicule. People would tell me it never happened, I was dreaming, or I needed a psychiatrist. This made me increasingly frustrated in my ability to testify to people. I appreciated that I had the disadvantage of being very ill and confined to a bed, but everyone (with a couple of exceptions) were completely antagonistic to the

Lessons Learned

possibility of Jesus and the angels being real. No clergy ever visited me. My religious affiliation was listed as none.

It was horrible to consider the possibility that my wife, children, and family might die without knowing Jesus and suffer the same fate I had known. When I tried to speak to them, they told me they didn't want to hear it. I prayed all the time that they would accept Jesus. During this time I became aware of the presence of demonic spirits drifting around visitors. The demons knew that I could see them, but the people they were attached to were oblivious to their presence. This was disturbing, and I would pray against them. I never told people about them because I knew they would not accept this. This ability to see demonic entities lasted for several months until I begged God to take that away from me. After I prayed I never saw them again, and I never want that ability to return. I lack the capacity to deal with them. I can only protect myself against them and advise others to do the same. The power in the name of Jesus is the force that protects me and defeats them.

The turning point in my recovery came with the intercession of two people. The first was a doctor who had just completed his training and residency. Dr Linne was called in by the group of doctors who were caring for me because they realized they were losing me after several weeks. He examined me very thoroughly and I

Lessons Learned

immediately responded to his spirit. He accepted without reservation my testimony, and I felt he was sympathetic to my condition. He admitted to me that I was critically ill, but he was going to do everything in his power to help me. No other doctor had been that honest with me. After he left, the nurses came in and took down all the bags of fluids I was receiving intravenously and replaced them with strange new bags of fluids. I learned Dr. Linne was giving me massive doses of the most recent and powerful antibiotics in the hope of stopping the infection. He risked killing me with an overdose of antibiotics, but saw the alternative as certain death from the infection. At this time my incision had burst open and copious amounts of foul smelling fluids were oozing out of my open wound. The thick bandages were changed every couple of hours saturated with this vile liquid. I was horrified by how repulsive this was when looking down at my body draining pus.

Within days, Dr. Linne's gamble started to have results and I was turning the corner toward recovery. The second person who was an instrument of God's grace was a lovely young nurse fresh form nursing school who worked the late night shift. Her name was Lisa, and she sometimes stayed in my room and listened to me talk about Jesus and the angels. She was happy to hear what I had to say. She understood my obsession with the

Lessons Learned

importance of love. At the time, I had not eaten any solids or liquids in weeks. This was contributing to my weakness. One night she brought me a milkshake she had made containing a protein supplement and real ice cream and told me to drink it. At first, I refused and accused her of trying to make me vomit. She told me she had made it with love and that she was going to stand there and watch me drink it all! I could not refuse her because I knew she had done this in love. It was delicious and I drank the whole thing. The next day I felt hunger for the first time in over a month. I asked my wife to bring me a hamburger and I devoured it. Lisa and Dr. Linne took risks to help me heal. They also listened without judgment.

There are three forces that must be involved and cooperating with healing. The patient has to be convinced of the medical staff's ability to heal and have no subconscious desire contrary to one's getting well. There could be many reasons hidden in the subconscious contributing to illness. The doctors, nurses, and caregivers are instruments of the "Great Physician" and they need to be inspired with compassion, sensitivity, and knowledge to do the work of Christ. Lastly the most important is the intervention of God in the healing. Given the catastrophic illness that I had, I would be dead if it were not for the intervention of God. God can do the miraculous, if people seek God's help. This means the whole team is on the

Lessons Learned

same page. When I came to the hospital in Kentucky, I was dying. It took time, but a godly healing team did come together and I got well rapidly.

During my illness I learned to pray hard, and it is likely I would have never learned to pray in any other way. I refused pain medication because it interfered with my ability to focus on prayer. All prayer is good, but some is better than others. Jesus told me about the importance of honesty in prayer. Hypocrisy in prayer nullifies the effectiveness of prayer. Being awkward and inarticulate are not impediments to prayer. Prayer can even be stillness and silence. Prayer can be raw emotion. Prayer can be ugly or beautiful – it makes no difference, as long as it is from the heart. Prayer is turning our attention to God and conversing and listening. When we turn our conscious attention to God it changes our lives in subtle ways. We become aware of what is important to us and we may become more conscious of God's will for us and the world. Prayer is not about changing God. That is absurd to consider. Prayer is about changing ourselves and the world's will. I have found the greatest aid to prayer is the book of Psalms. In that book are one hundred and fifty excellent prayers. One can use the psalms to lead people in prayer. If you need a place to start, the twenty-third psalm is a perfect prayer and can easily be memorized. Jesus taught his disciples a perfect

Lessons Learned

and simple prayer. There are countless examples of prayer for us to use and to learn from. The best thing about being ill is that it both affords you the opportunity to pray and it motivates you to pray. I am thankful for that blessing of being dependent on prayer. I have had many prayers answered and I have had prayers that did not result in the outcome I wished for at the time. I am convinced all prayer is answered, but our prayers are not always answered the way we would have things to be. I urge you to pray for anything, everything, all the time, any way you can, and let God be God.

As I began to recover from my illness, which was a process that took over a year, I learned many valuable lessons. One of those lessons was gratitude. When nothing enters your throat for days and you finally have a sip of water, it is an amazing sensation. I want to be grateful for every drink. Food is not only necessary for life but it is also a pleasure and we should be grateful and express our gratitude to God for our food and the people who provide it. I enjoy thanking God for a meal and have never regretted saying a prayer in a public setting at the meal. In fact, strangers have told me they appreciated seeing us pray in public. We pray quietly and discreetly in public and are not attempting to attract attention, but, we are not ashamed of expressing gratitude for the meal.

Lessons Learned

The more you pray the more natural it becomes. One can feel self-conscious at first until you can just go into that zone where the prayer flows from the heart. When I became a pastor I was very nervous about praying publically. Now I find that it is a blessing to have the opportunity to be asked to pray publically. Praying is not a show of piety and should never be used for that purpose. Prayer is connecting to God, and that is all that matters.

We are all imperfect people and sin in our thoughts, words, and deeds. God not only knows that, but totally understands our deficiencies because God knows us intimately and He lived among us. God does not expect perfection, but God does expect our best efforts to avoid sin. The appropriate attitude is to ground our prayers in praise of God and include confession of our sins to God, repentance from our sins and mistakes, and petition for gifts to improve in our relationship to God and our brothers and sisters. God wants to give us the good gifts of the Holy Spirit if we can be used for the Body of Christ. Prayer is our direct link to God.

Lessons Learned

Lessons Learned

1. God speaks to us if we listen. How well are we listening to God? If we hear God speaking do we believe and do we follow what God is telling us to do?
2. Sometimes following God involved risks. God challenges us to give up control and security for a better life, if we are willing to let go, and let God be our God.
3. People called into the healing vocations can be instruments of God's miraculous healings. They also may take risks to follow God in order to heal.
4. Suffering is an important opportunity for learning and spiritual growth. When we are being tested we can find new resources for building our relationship with God. Prayer is one of our links to God. We both speak and listen to God in prayer.
5. Gratitude is one of the most important qualities we must cultivate in ourselves. Suffering is essential to learning gratitude for everything we have been given by God in this life.

Chapter 8 – Learning to Walk

There was a big grey recliner in the family room of our house, and that became my permanent settled place during the months of recovery. It was next to a large window that faced the east which bathed the room in serious sunlight during the day. From the time that I got up in the morning to the time I went to bed, I lived in that heavily cushioned chair. My wife went to work, and our two children left for school so I had the luxury of peace and quiet to read and pray. I had missed my dog because I had been in the hospital for two months and had not seen her. She stayed by my side all the time and was very sensitive to the fact that I was fragile. I had lost seventy pounds and was extremely weak. To get up and go to the bathroom was a major feat, and I would take a long rest to recuperate from the effort. I was delighted to be thinner than I had been since tenth grade and imagined that I would not gain the weight back. I avoided looking in the mirror because my eyes were bright orange and scary. My skin was very jaundiced and not attractive. I knew that I was a completely different person on the inside and wished I would be a completely different person on the outside to show that I had changed totally.

My eyesight came back, and I was constantly reading the Bible. To my delight, not only did it make sense to me, but

Lessons Learned

it was speaking directly to me. Many of the things Jesus had taught me were written in the Bible. I fell in love with the Word of God. When my wife and children came home, I was excited to read to them and tell them about what I had found in the Bible. At first they tolerated these Bible lessons to humor me, but they soon resisted the lectures. The more they resisted the more impatient I became with them. From my perspective these words from Scripture were the inspired words of God speaking to us. They, however, did not appreciate what I was trying to share with them. They rejected my attempts to evangelize them. I was painfully aware that the father and husband they had known all their lives was now a stranger to them. Everything I had been, I now was opposite. The Christianity I had ridiculed was now all I cared about and desperately wanted them to accept. The fun things we enjoyed were now strictly forbidden. I now hated heavy metal music, dirty jokes, blasphemy, pornography, derogatory statements about people, greed, most television programs, professional sports, alcoholic drinks, and so on. They did not like this new man and his strict taboos and ardor for the Bible. I couldn't comprehend how repulsive I was to them!

When I read the Bible it thrilled me with its wisdom and the presence of God in the words written on those pages that spoke to me. How was it possible that they couldn't

Lessons Learned

sense the importance and truth of what I was reading and speaking to them? The Scriptures confirmed, clarified, and gave authority to what I had undergone in my near-death experience. The gulf between my family and me was widening, and I was in tears about their rejection of God's invitation to have a relationship with them through Jesus Christ. My family began to avoid me as much as they possibly could. From their perspective I had become a raving lunatic who lived all day in a chair, dressed in a bathrobe, and was obsessed with Jesus. One night my wife told me she was going to leave and take our children because she couldn't take the lectures about the Bible any more. I begged her not to leave me. She insisted her mind was made up. The only way I could convince her to stay was to promise to stop speaking about the Bible and God anymore. By repeating that promise several times, she finally agreed to stay.

This agreement conflicted me to the core of my being. I had raised and influenced my wife and children to be and think the way they were, and now I wanted to undo the damage that I had done, and give them a different understanding of life. They were living with a Bible thumping fanatic. Earlier when I had awoken from surgery in Paris, I knew that my wife and children were in danger by our rejection of God. The authority of the Holy Bible did not impress them in the least. My passion and love for

Lessons Learned

God turned them off. My prayers were not affecting them. I knew I was responsible for their hard hearts which kept them from any interest in changing. The three of them were in agreement and they hoped I would get over it and return to the person I had been.

During this time, my wife told me twice, "The man I married died in Paris, and you are a total stranger to me."

"You're right" I told her, "but I love you more than ever. When you know Jesus, you can love more than you ever imagined."

This wasn't the answer she hoped to hear. We had been married twenty years at this point. Her career as an attorney was just beginning and she had joined a law firm composed of people who were her peers and they were beginning to be very successful. She was working long hours, seven days a week. While at home, I – her husband – was lying in a recliner all day, dressed in a bathrobe, and reading the Bible. I was trying to regain my health so that I could return to the hospital to have major abdominal surgery to rebuild my abdomen. The peritonitis had dissolved abdominal muscles, and I had adhesions and scarifications around my organs. The faster I got strong enough, the sooner I could have surgery and get back to life. After two weeks at home, we went out for the first time to see one of the doctors. On the way to the doctor's

Lessons Learned

office I asked my wife if she had ever heard of a song that had the line "I once was lost and now am found. I once had died and now I live?" She began to sing "Amazing Grace" to me. I cried all the way to the doctor's office. I kept repeating to her, "This was my song!" Decades later it is still my song! My wife was worried that I would make a scene at the doctor's office and embarrass her. I tried to not embarrass her and didn't talk about Jesus.

After several more weeks I told her I wanted to try walking, so that evening we drove to the University because there was a big, flat, faculty-only parking lot that would be mostly vacant. I walked about fifty feet and then walked back to the car. I told her, one day I'm going walk a mile. Many nights we went to the campus and she accompanied me, walking around the parking lots. Every time we would go a little farther. Years before, when I was a teenager, I started lifting weights daily. I had become the best shot-putter and discus thrower in my high school by my sophomore year. My present back yard has hundreds of feet of stone walls that I laid by myself. I gathered most of the stone from along the highways and hauled them home in my pickup truck. I built my house from the fountain to the roof. My point here is to verify that I was very strong and that much of my identity was about my strength and independence. I hated to ask for help from anyone. To lose one's image of being a

Lessons Learned

"superman" to being weaker than a kitten was a struggle. I had had much pride in being superior to other people, and now I was learning to walk like a baby. God works in mysterious ways, and I'm thankful to God that I have been humbled. I can no longer pretend I'm the "baddest bear" in the woods. I can't bully or intimidate anyone. I need to ask for help and I am reliant on other people. God has given me many friends that I love and trust.

While recovering from my illness at home, I rarely had visitors. The people whom I considered my friends did not come to see me, with a couple of exceptions. The man that had visited me at the hospital came by to see me when I returned home. I told him a brief description of what I had experienced in Paris. He listened without comment and left when I finished my story. I later found out from my wife that he called her and told her she needed to divorce me because I had lost my mind. He has never spoken to me since. Another person that I thought was a close friend told me that I had a morphine-induced hallucination and that I should forget about it. That was particularly insulting since I had begged for hours in the French Hospital for any medication without success. I asked God why I was losing everybody. God responded by telling me that I would have new friends, and more than I could know. I found that God was not mistaken.

Lessons Learned

While I became engrossed in the Bible, I decided that I needed to check out other religions to compare them to the Judeo–Christian faith I was discovering. I purchased the Koran, the Bhagavad-Gita, a collection of Buddhist Texts, Bahia scriptures, and other religious materials and read them. I found them interesting, but they did not compare to the Bible. The Bible is not comparable to any other literature. If it is read prayerfully, the Holy Spirit speaks to the reader and reveals truth and wisdom that has been inspired into the words. You can read a passage many times over the years and learn new truths from it. Without the guidance of the Holy Spirit, the Bible is confusing and legalistic. With the Spirit of Christ the Bible is freeing and opens the mind to discovery.

After rehabilitating at home for a few months, I became ambulatory to a very limited degree. I was eager to go to church, but I had no notion of where to go. I hadn't attended a church in my adult life. I consulted the yellow pages and found hundreds of churches. I prayed that God would show me a church in the phone book, but nothing happened. Then I found an advertisement for a church half an hour away that looked appealing so I asked my wife to take me there. When we went to the location we found it was closed for the summer. I was confused. A few days later I got a phone call from an art teacher inviting me to her church in the town I lived in. I asked my wife if

Lessons Learned

she knew the church. She said she had been there for concerts when my daughter was in the high school choir and it seemed nice. So I asked her if she would take me there on Sunday. That Sunday came and I got up early to shower, shave and put on a suit and tie. I wanted to make a good impression because I was fearful they would see me for what I had been. I knew I was a terrible sinner who had been forgiven by Jesus, but would they forgive me? I thought the people in church must be saints and I would stand out as a fallen man.

My wife parked in the bank parking lot across from the church and we had to walk fifty yards across the street into the church. I was exhausted by the time we climbed the few steps into the church. The worship service had begun and the congregation was singing the opening hymn, "A Mighty Fortress is Our God." As we walked a few steps into the church I looked up and saw the angels. There were hundreds of golden angels hovering in the ceiling smiling at the congregation's worship. Out of respect and awe for the presence of the angels, I immediately dropped to the floor and prostrated myself praising God. Since this was not a Pentecostal church and this type of behavior was not customary, two ushers came to my aid and tried to lift me up. I resisted their help because I was doing what I believed to be appropriate in the presence of a host of angels. My wife bent over and

Lessons Learned

told me to stop making a fool of myself, and to get up. After several minutes of lying flat on the floor moaning praises to God I allowed the ushers to lift me up and deposit me into the nearest pew.

The people around us tried not to stare at me, but I didn't really care what the people thought because I was interested in the angels. My wife whispered to me she had never been so embarrassed in all of her life and we would never go to church again. I cried through the entire service. I had trouble following the getting-up and the sitting-down. My wife would try to show me where we were in the liturgy and hymnals but I couldn't follow because I was in awe of the angels and the intensity of the Spirit I felt inside of me and in that worship of God. My wife rushed us out of there as soon as the benediction was said. She made it clear we would never go to church again.

During the following week I continually promised her I would behave in church and that I had to go back. She finally gave in and we went to church the next Sunday. I was excited all week to go back to church. As far as I was concerned, it had been the highlight of my life! To my delight, the people at the church did not judge me and they were friendly and greeted us warmly. I met the pastor and he said he would like to visit us. The following week he came to our house during the day. I told him

Lessons Learned

about my near death experience and he listened. When I was finished he said that he hoped I would come to a class he was starting for new Christians to learn more about the church. I was thrilled to be invited. When I told my wife about the classes, she refused to attend, but she agreed to drive me to the classes.

The pastor gave us lectures on the background of the church and the denomination which was the United Church of Christ. He told us about the sacraments and elements of worship. After several weeks he asked us to pair up with another person he selected and to share our first experience of God with each other. He paired me with a woman in her eighties who attended the classes with her husband. He was almost deaf and she had repeated everything the pastor said loudly in his ear. After weeks of this I found her to be quite annoying. When I asked her to tell me when she had first known there was a God, she said she couldn't talk to me. I asked her, "Why?" She said she was uneducated and knew I was a college professor and couldn't talk to me. I told her the pastor had told us to do this so she had to speak to me and I wanted to hear what she had to say. She told me she had always known God and always felt God close to her. I asked her if she had ever been afraid. She said she had never been afraid because God was with her. She left me speechless. I was so proud of the fact that I had found

Lessons Learned

God recently and here was a woman who had known God all of her life. I told her I was honored to know her. After that I admired her for telling her husband what was going on.

The pastor and I became close friends and we had many good conversations. I became his confidant and learned more about the church than I wanted to know. The people at Christ Church were really good people and made me feel accepted even though they knew nothing about me. I was surprised at how readily they allowed me to become part of their community. After a few months I joined the church. My wife attended Sunday worship with me, but under duress. I threatened her with divorce if she didn't attend. I was hoping that she would be converted by attending church since she had forbidden me to evangelize her. Meanwhile, my children refused to attend and my wife supported them in their decision. Every Sunday I was elated by the worship and every Sunday my wife would criticize the service. She wanted me to know how she suffered attending church.

It was evident from the beginning that the church was seeking the truth about God and who we are. I wanted to know more about God and the revelation of God in the Bible, and here and I had found a whole community of people close to my home who were seeking the same thing! I had presumed the church was composed of

Lessons Learned

people who thought they were saints and all acted holier than thou. What I found was very different from that attitude. I found ordinary people who where acutely aware of their sin and had found redemption from sin through Jesus Christ. They knew the love of God in their own way, and sought ways to express that love. The congregation ranged from the mayor to the cafeteria lady, and everyone had a love and concern for each other. The church was not perfect, but it was the most loving community I had ever known.

In October I was sufficiently rehabilitated to have the surgery that was necessary. Facing the surgery with the knowledge that I had the prayers and support of my church made me confident I would not have any problems. The surgeon informed he would be implanting a large synthetic mesh in my abdomen to take the place of the muscles that had been lost due to the peritonitis. He anticipated the surgery lasting four hours. My friend, Sister Dolores, had given me a rosary that she had made and I wanted to take that with me into surgery. I prayed that God would give me a sign that I belonged to God. I didn't know what that sign might be but I prayed for it to happen in any way that God chose. I wrapped the rosary around my hand as I was wheeled into pre-op. A masked woman approached me and asked, "Howard, how are you?" By the tone of her voice I knew she was someone I

Lessons Learned

knew, but I couldn't recognize her because of the surgical mask.

"It's Jean from church," she said.

I was so relieved because she was one of my favorite people at church. She told me she would be with me during the entire surgery. Then she noticed the rosary. She told me I couldn't have the rosary around my hand. I told her it had to come with me. She said that she knew what to do. She removed the rosary wrapped around my hand and put it in a plastic bag and slipped it under my back. She said it would be with me during the surgery.

After the surgery the doctor said that it was the most amazing surgery he had ever done. He said the muscles came together in ways that he had not thought were possible and he did not have to use the plastic mesh. He said he had never had a surgery like it. A few days later the surgeon came in and removed the huge bandage that covered my entire abdomen. When he pulled it off, I could hardly believe it. The incision was a large cross in my abdomen. I felt I had received the sign from God that I'd prayed for before the surgery. Now I have a ten inch cross carved into my skin that will be with me for the rest of my life. The mark of the cross reminds me that I belong to Jesus Christ.

Lessons Learned

Lessons Learned

1. The Bible is the "living word of God" and completely unique in all literature. To understand and learn the wisdom of God, one must have the Holy Spirit to open up the meaning of Scriptures.
2. Those who do not have the Holy Spirit cannot understand or appreciate the Word of God in the Bible. This can create tremendous strife between family members and between friends. Becoming an enthusiastic Christian appears to be madness to those who don't have the Spirit of Christ in their hearts.
3. During our life, we build an ego-identity that too often becomes an obstacle to spiritual growth and maturity. It is common that this ego must be shattered in order for further growth to occur. A catastrophe may be the best thing that happens to us for the sake of real advancement towards heaven.
4. The church is the "Body of Christ," and it was created by Jesus Christ for our Christian discipleship. God will lead us to the church if we pray and seek the guidance of the Holy Spirit.
5. The church is not a spectator sport. It is through participation in the work of the church that one can

Lessons Learned

know Jesus more fully and serve our sisters and brothers in Christ.

Lessons Learned

Chapter 9 – Sharing the Story

When I returned to teaching at the University in January I was excited to connect with students. Teaching art to college students could not be more fun. The students are interesting and usually motivated because art is not a practical career path. I didn't talk about my conversion in the classroom, but the word was getting around that I had changed. Students were seeking me out for counseling, and it was a privilege to try to advise them. My life was very content between teaching and church activities.

For weeks I had been praying about world hunger. I asked God to show me a way to be involved in caring for those without adequate food. One day in church a woman spoke about her recent experience serving at a local food kitchen on Saturday. After her brief narrative about her preparing a meal and feeding the poor, she asked for volunteers for the next Saturday. After the service was over I went to her and told her I would be interested in serving at the soup kitchen. She gave me the information of when and where to go on Saturday. When I arrived early in the morning at the old church building in a depressed part of Cincinnati, the doors were locked. After a while some people showed up and let me into the building. I met the pastor who showed us few volunteers how to slice the bologna, make sandwiches, and heat the

Lessons Learned

canned soup. After a couple of hours we had a few hundred sandwiches and several gallons of soup ready to transport to another location. We loaded everything into a van and drove several miles to the toughest neighborhood in Cincinnati. We unloaded the food into the first floor of an old building which was the site of the soup kitchen. We proceeded to serve three hundred people in one hour. One of the more experienced volunteers asked me if I was there because of middle-class guilt. I told him I was just looking for a way to help the poor. The people whom we served were very diverse and consistently polite and thankful. The food was very simple and they ate with relish. This small effort to feed hundreds of people was exactly what I had prayed for, and I felt like my prayer had been answered. The next Saturday I showed up early in the morning at the mission church to help prepare the food for the soup kitchen. I worked there every Saturday for the next five years, until it was not possible for me to do it anymore.

After months of working at the kitchen I was put in charge of procuring the food and donations, recruiting volunteers, preparing the food, and serving our guests. I found sources of produce who would donate cases of fresh fruits and vegetables that were no longer saleable. I would fill my pickup truck with donations during the week for the meal. I found sources of meat and poultry that I

Lessons Learned

could buy wholesale. We changed the menu from sandwiches to a full meal with choices to offer our guests. The people appreciated having choices of good food. Cooking for several hundred people from scratch required many volunteers and it became necessary to recruit two or three dozen people every week. Happily, it was not difficult contacting churches and getting volunteers. Soon we had many people who helped regularly on Saturdays and knew what to do and how to train new recruits.

Over time I got to know many of our regular clients and listened to their stories. Everyone had reasons why they were eating at the soup kitchen. If there were freeloaders and cheaters there, I never met them. The people I talked with were good people who had severe health problems, mental disabilities, or unemployment. None of them wanted to be coming to a soup kitchen, but they came because they were trying to survive. With a little help they could have become independent and wouldn't have needed a soup kitchen. I wasn't able to give them the counseling they required to get back on their feet. We were able to give them a meal, which they appreciated and needed. I tried to treat them with respect and be interested in their lives. It was especially rewarding to bring volunteers from the suburbs and give them the opportunity to meet and serve inner-city residents. This changed some attitudes about the poor. Many times

Lessons Learned

volunteers told me they realized they were no different from the people we served except that they'd had some misfortune in their lives. It made the volunteers more grateful for what they had. Working at the soup kitchen was very satisfying for me and I never wanted to give it up, but circumstances forced me to do other things.

At the University, the department chair resigned and there was an election and I was elected to be the Art Department chairperson. I had done this for several years, earlier, and was an obvious candidate for the job. This position meant I would be working twelve months a year and there was a substantial increase in salary. The main reason I took the position was that I thought I could have a positive influence on the program, faculty, and students alike. There had been serious strife going on in the art department and I hoped to bring harmony to the situation and further the department's growth. Chairing a group of art professors is like trying to herd cats. I loved the eccentricity of artists, but found their egocentricity a challenge. There was only one other Christian among the art faculty, but that wasn't a problem for me because I had dealt with artists all my life. I felt it was my task to represent Christ-like behavior toward everyone.

At the end of the spring semester when it was time for me to take over as Chairperson, the secretary resigned and I needed to hire a secretary. My wife and I were going on a

Lessons Learned

two week vacation before my new position began and I was going out of town precisely when it was time to interview and hire the secretary. I had to leave the responsibility for hiring the secretary to the personnel office of the university. While on vacation, I prayed fervently God would send me a Christian secretary.

When I returned I met Janet Neltner who had been hired to be my secretary. My first day back, I introduced myself and mentioned I was a spiritual person. Looking at her reaction, I knew she didn't know how to respond to that. That evening I had a meeting at church and told a woman about my new secretary, and expressed my hope that she was a Christian. The woman asked me what her name was. When I told her, she laughed. She said I had the strongest Christian in the entire county. They were old friends. The next day I told my new secretary that I found out she was a Christian, and I knew that we were going to get along very well. We became close friends and we had good times working together for several years. We are still good friends.

My office became a place where students would come for counseling. Students from all over the campus came by to talk about their lives. Clearly, there was an unfilled need on campus for students to have a sympathetic advisor. I kept a Bible on my desk, but I was not trying to evangelize. The dean of the college of liberal arts called

Lessons Learned

me to his office. He warned me not to mention God, Jesus, the Bible, religion, or church to any of the students. It was his opinion that mentioning religion in the classroom would be a violation of the separation of church and state, and that would expose the university to a lawsuit. I meekly sat there and assured him I would never do such a thing. At the time, I didn't know why he felt it was necessary to threaten me because I had never talked about faith in a classroom. I can only assume the rumors about my conversion made me suspect.

I regret that I accepted my dean's warning seriously. This is one of the lies propagated by atheists to silence faith in higher education. The university loudly proclaims the importance of academic freedom and freedom of speech. But that doesn't apply to anything about God, Jesus, Christianity, or church unless one is ridiculing them. Many students have been exposed to professors who frequently demean Christianity in the classroom even when it had nothing to do with the subject of the class. It is too often open season on putting down the Christian faith all over the academic community, and that is defended as academic freedom. Professors are warned not to speak in support of Christianity and the threats are not subtle. What kind of freedom of speech is this? The shameful truth is people believe there is a law against speaking about faith. There is no such law expect in the minds of atheists. I regret I was so stupid as to believe in this lie and censor myself. There are teachers who practice sorcery, are hedonists, pagans, drunkards, anarchists, communists, nihilists, existentialists, etc., and they openly profess their beliefs. What a scandal it is if a professor speaks about his or her Christian faith at a public university! How many thousands, or possibly millions of young Christians have been influenced by their professors to leave the Christian faith?

I wish I were exaggerating about what is going on in public higher education, but I am not. When I was student, I was heavily influenced by an atheist professor. My twenty years at the university were divided between my years as a Christ-basher and my years as a follower of Jesus. This is a spiritual battleground for the hearts, minds, and souls of our youth. The atheists may be a small minority of the population, but they have won the university. The fact is: Christianity is a joke to many in academia.

The contrast between the hypocrisy of the academic world and the honesty of the church pulled me apart. I had spent my entire life studying, practicing, loving, and living art. Being an artist was my identity and joy. The church is far from perfect and declining in prestige and influence in our society. As a tenured full professor and department chair, I was making an excellent wage, had status in society, enjoyed a growing pension (and could

Lessons Learned

look forward to a comfortable retirement), and I loved the students. By every standard I had it made, and only had to continue doing what I was trained and competent to do for another decade or two, and then could retire. When I talked to my wife about the possibility of going into Christian ministry, she became very angry. Those conversations were brief. I, myself, wondered if I was delusional in thinking God was calling me to the ministry.

The more involved I became in the work of the church, the more I loved it. I enrolled in a three-year training program for visiting and ministering to the sick and shut-ins. At the conclusion of that program I was ordained as a lay minister. Along with weekly pastoral visits, running a soup kitchen on Saturdays, teaching Sunday school, leading a healing service on Tuesday nights, helping with the youth group, and doing maintenance work around the church, I was studying Christian literature and attending numerous retreats. This church activity was outside of my fulltime work at the university. The pastor started using me as a liturgist during worship and eventually he asked me to preach sermons more and more. I was feeling called to the ministry. In 1988, I told my wife I wanted to take a class at a seminary. She was opposed to the idea, but said she couldn't stop me. My plan was to take one class to test the response I would have to seminary

Lessons Learned

education, for I knew seminary education was a necessary first step in preparation for ministry.

My denomination requires a process of interviews and testing for consideration for ordained ministry. The head of the ordination committee tried to discourage me from going into the ministry. He told me I should be content with being an active lay person. He said I would be of more service to the church if I stayed at the university and served the church on Sundays. He also told other people that the church did not need people like me. I chose to attend a Methodist seminary in Dayton, Ohio. United Theological Seminary is seventy miles from my home and was the closest accredited protestant seminary. I was required to take a three-day examination by a psychologist in Columbus, Ohio, in order to determine my suitability for ministry. The psychologist gave me approval for ordination for ministry. My first class at seminary that met at night convinced me I wanted more learning. I was facing three to four years of fulltime study at the graduate level to obtain my Master of Divinity degree which is required for ordination. The other requirement was to serve different churches as a student pastor. I would have to be a fulltime graduate student, serve a church, and continue chairing the art department. My wife was not supportive of this decision. Seminary was expensive and I got little financial support from my church.

Lessons Learned

At seminary, we took classes in theology, biblical studies, and ministry. The other seminarians were wonderful people who were all at different stages of exploring their call to ministry. Of the ninety people with whom we began, about sixty completed the program. There were many students from different denominations. The majority were Methodists. We made close friends in seminary and supported each other. Because of my education from Jesus, I was well prepared in my theological understanding. Additionally, I had been reading and studying for several years prior to seminary. I thrived in this environment and would have been happy to have spent the rest of my life in seminary, learning about Christianity. Because of my hectic schedule, I was rarely home and my family didn't complain about my absence. If they felt abandoned by me, they didn't express that feeling to me.

Working during the day at the university, I became increasingly aware of the hostility I sensed in my colleagues about what I considered sacred. Trying to serve them in Christian love was fine with them because they would take everything I could give. However, there was a dilemma for me. Their values and mine were not compatible. The students, on the other hand, were a delight and yet I was constrained in giving them what they really needed. My extensive counseling in the privacy of

Lessons Learned

my office was not part of my job description, and even there I felt limited in how much faith I could share. The few other Christian faculty I met kept their faith separate from their positions as professors. They appeared to live two separate identities. It was increasingly impossible for me to do this. More and more my calling was to serve God by serving the Body of Christ.

By this time in my early forties, I had enough life experience so that I had no illusions about the church. But what was the alternative to a dysfunctional church? The church was composed of human beings and they brought all of their beauty and ugliness into communal life. They came with all of their brilliance and foolishness. The church is similar to every other institution with which I had been involved, except that there are moments of the sublime presence of God in the church. That was when the Holy Spirit was taking charge. So, ministry consisted of managing the mundane responsibilities of being human, punctuated with miraculous moments of transformation.

Serving as a student pastor gave me the opportunity to become more involved in the lives of people of different congregations into which I was placed. The distinct quality of the people I worked with was their desire to live lives pleasing to God, as they understood what that might mean. How well they achieved that goal varied widely, but the fact they intentionally were striving toward God

Lessons Learned

made them attractive to me. They were doing precisely what I was doing. How does one live a life pleasing to God? This would be a futile pursuit if it were not for a few critical factors. We have a tradition of sacred literature collected in the Bible which informs us of the history of the human pursuit of understanding God, and we have God inspiring people with God's self-revelation. We have the traditions of the Judeo-Christian centuries during which people were struggling to be the people of God. We have the guidance of the Holy Spirit to correct us and lead us in our journey. Most importantly we have a relationship with Jesus Christ who is a real presence in our lives. So we struggle onward battling the lower human instincts to respond to the divinity we are called to become.

It is vanity to think of oneself as the worst sinner in the world. We are all sinners and have betrayed God horribly. The unique feature of Christianity is that we acknowledge our sinfulness and know we have been forgiven our sins by Jesus who died on the cross. When I stand before a congregation to lead them in worship, I am profoundly aware that I am not worthy to be there. I know I am not a good person and have no right to pretend otherwise. The only reason I can perform my function as pastor is to know that I have been forgiven and that God has called me to build up the Body of Christ. It is a comfort to know that the disciples of Jesus and all His followers for the past two thousand years were also sinners called to be the Body of Christ. I am no better and no worse than any of them. God uses us for God's good purpose for those who love God.

My overarching concern has been to be authentic as a person. I have always had an aversion to hypocrisy. This began with my childhood and has grown more acute as the years go by. As a pastor, I never wanted to pretend to be something I was not. My best friend was Rev Jim Willig, a Catholic priest. He was an extremely popular priest in Cincinnati who died several years ago. For more than a decade I had the privilege of being a close friend of his. When he preached, there was often standing room only in his parish. There were numerous occasions when I studied his preaching and other interactions with his congregations. What I discovered was that the quality that people loved in him was his authenticity. He was completely transparent and real. When he preached, people related to his humanity and his passionate love of God. He was the best preacher I ever heard and the finest man I have known. What a blessing he was to me! And I thank God that I knew him. He blessed everyone who knew him. I can only hope to aspire to be more like him.

Lessons Learned

Lessons Learned

1. The Spirit of Christ opens our hearts to compassion, and especially love of the poor. Serving the poor is a blessing to the server and to those being served. In Christian service we are following Jesus.
2. We are not alone in our Christian faith. God will send brothers and sisters in Christ to guide us and support us even in secular work if we pray for help.
3. Many people are hostile to Christianity and they seek ways to silence Christians and marginalize them at work and in society. Freedom of speech and freedom of religion are denied Christians and must be asserted in every segment of society.
4. God calls every follower of Christ to greater involvement in building the church and furthering the Kingdom of God in this world. God wants us to be well equipped and prepared for our ministry. The call demands perseverance, time, and sacrifice.
5. Jesus called ordinary men and women to be his disciples. Jesus calls people like you and me to be His instrument of bringing salvation and justice to the entire world. We are a royal priesthood.

Chapter 10 – Talking and Talking

Why the need to talk about what had happened? It is a compulsion. I want to tell everyone about my discovery of something extremely important. It is comparable to wanting to share a vast treasure with everyone. And it is also driven by the urgency of seeing people heading for a cliff when they are completely unaware of what is before them. It contains equal amounts of wanting to give away something precious and to warn of possible disaster. Life would have been much simpler if there was not this need to talk about my experience, but it has been my responsibility to talk about it when asked - to anyone, anywhere, and at any time. It has not always been convenient or fun. It has never produced income and has often been costly. I cannot deny the tendency to feel embarrassment on some of those occasions; I am well aware that many people consider me a fool or a fake. But that is not a deterrent to my being who I am. I think of myself as a wretch who was saved.

When I first started to tell my story, I experienced such intense emotions that I was overwhelmed to the point that I was only able to speak a few sentences. It was exhausting experiencing those powerful feelings again. I

Lessons Learned

tried for years to distance myself from the emotions that I experienced so that I wouldn't suffer the feelings I experienced. How many times people would say, "It's okay if you cry." It was not okay for me because it was really painful for me. The near death experience (NDE) is unique in that it never fades. Memories fade, dreams vanish, and the highlights of life are forgotten, but the NDE remains as vivid decades later, as if it happened today. It is the only experience I have had that has left an indelible impression. The problem for me is not remembering it; rather, the problem is how to distance myself enough from the experience in order to be able to talk about it without becoming emotionally overwhelmed.

There are two very different parts to my NDE. The negative part of the experience I would gladly forget, but I cannot. The glorious time I spent with Jesus I think about often, and wish I could never lose the feelings of His love for a single moment.

After a few months back at the University, one of my students told me there was a psychology professor that was studying near death experiences and he would like to meet me. Professor Scott Quimby and I met and found we had a mutual interest in NDEs. He told me about a group that met monthly in a church in Cincinnati. They were associated with the International Association for Near Death Studies – also known as IANDS. I went to the

Lessons Learned

meeting and immediately connected to the church's charming pastor and his wife who attended these meetings regularly. There were about thirty people at the meeting and a few had had NDE's. It was most reaffirming for me to speak to a group of people who were not only interested in, but also accepted near death experiences without reservation. I attended those meetings regularly until the time I went to seminary. It was healing to support and be supported by others' experiences. It was also a place where we could speak about our experiences openly and honestly. I made several good friends at those meetings.

I began meeting regularly for lunch with a man in his late seventies to discuss theology and cosmology. At one of our meetings he told me to not write a book because he believed it would be interpreted by some people as my effort to exploit the experience for profit. He was certain my credibility would be questioned if I wrote a book; it would appear I was of trying to make money from it. He gave me this warning because many people were encouraging me to write a book so they could share my story with others. Scott Quimby was very interested in me publishing my story and we often talked about the possibility. In fact, Scott began taping interviews with me as possible source for a book. After the warning about writing a book my enthusiasm waned, and I eventually

Lessons Learned

decided I would not write a book. Another friend, Ed Riess, was duplicating tape cassettes of a talk I had given and was sending them free to anyone who asked for one. He gave away hundreds of tapes and kept me supplied with hundreds more to give away. That went on for more than two decades. Ed supplied me with a fast tape duplicator and I was buying tapes by the caseload. I sent free tapes out until there was no more demand for cassette tapes. I seriously investigated how to publish a book and give it away for free. Unfortunately, I could not afford the expense of doing that. During this time, many more people told me I should write a book.

In 1999 I told God I would write a book if He would give me a specific sign that He wanted me to publish my story. I went so far as to mention to God that a clear sign would be for a publisher to contact me to write the book. Within days of my prayer to God for a sign, I got a call from a publisher. He was in England and he asked me to write my story, and he assured me he would publish it. I agreed, and he sent me a contract, which I signed and returned to him. I asked permission from my church to take Fridays and Saturdays off so that I could write my book. They agreed.

I wrote a chapter a day and worked on it other days when I had some free time; it was finished in ten weeks. I wrote it without sharing any of it with anyone except a woman

Lessons Learned

who kindly offered to edit it. I sent the finished copy to the publisher in England and he was satisfied with the results. The publisher didn't like the title so we negotiated a title change. He also changed the order of the chapters. The book was published in paperback in England in 2000. It sold well and became the publisher's best seller. The man ran a small publishing house and sold ten thousand copies the first year. This was extraordinary for him. This was gratifying, but the book was not available in the United States except by ordering it from England. Five years later I was asked by the author, Anne Rice, if I would be interested in having the book published in the United States. I was excited to have that happen and in a matter of a few days I had a contract with Doubleday publishers.

Sometimes I get inquiries from new authors about advice on how to get a book published. They must think I am being uncooperative when I tell them I prayed and a publisher contacted me. The truth is, that all I know about publishing. This book has happened the same way.

I thought about putting a statement in the books about any profits being used for mission work in Central America. The publisher did not like the idea so it was excluded. For thirteen years the book generated several thousands of dollars a year, and all of that money (and more of my income) has gone to support the mission work I have been engaged in. I could not use income

Lessons Learned

earned from the book about my experience of salvation for myself so I gave it all away. There have been times when I needed the money to pay bills, but I couldn't bring myself to use it that way.

The same principle is true with offerings that I have been given after speaking at churches or groups. I have never charged a fee and have only accepted travel expenses. I don't do this to impress people because only my wife has known about this. I do this because I want to please God and give to God what God has given to me. My only regret is that my book has only sold eighty thousand copies in fifteen years. If it had sold more I could have done so much more in the missions we led in Belize. The hardest part of spending time with the poor is having so little resources to help with their needs.

The unforeseen result of the sending of tapes and publication of the book has been the requests for interviews from television and radio shows. I have never solicited any of these, and have no knowledge of how they became aware of me. There have been many interviews over the years. They have often been rebroadcast years later. These interviews now appear on the internet, the source of many of these programs on YouTube. I don't know how they get there, but it is gratifying that someone is interested enough to share them. As a consequence of the internet, many people

Lessons Learned

contact me daily seeking advice, asking questions, and making comments. It has been difficult at times to keep up with the volume of emails because it requires hours every day. My intention is to prayerfully and simply respond to every one. On rare occasions, it feels more appropriate to not respond since I do not want to engage with the person. The reason that motivates me to continue this ministry is that there are individuals who appreciate the answers I give them. It frequently occurs to me that there are a lot of people in the world who need to speak with a pastor, and I wonder why they have sought me out.

I have to take the e-mails seriously because there is no way to know the sincerity of these people. They reveal what they wish for me to know about them, and no more. I will probably never meet them or even hear back from them. They are complete strangers to me asking every kind of question. I hope and pray to respond appropriately. Over the years there have been thousands of these contacts, and with the help of God, I have done some good by responding. It is absolutely true that I am not in a position to fix these people, or even change them, but I try to direct them to the One who can help them and make a big difference in their lives. When I sense a person is honestly seeking God, I try to prayerfully respond to them.

Lessons Learned

Over time I have learned to have very low expectations about my ability to influence anyone, but I have also learned to have unlimited expectations about what God can do if the person is willing to let God be their God.

When my wife left me, I fell into a deep depression and I was encouraged to attend Al Anon. My situation was critical, and Al Anon helped me better understand my own diseased thinking, my role in the marital dynamics, and the work of the Holy Spirit. Listening to other people speak about their situations greatly increased my understanding of what I was going through. Having the opportunity to express my problems to a group of people, who easily knew the same circumstances, made solutions more apparent. In some respects I believe Al Anon saved my life. I was attending a meeting every day for months. Despair and depression thrives in secrecy and darkness, and talking openly about our situation brings light and love into the gloom and dispels the depression. Al Anon is free and has no professional staff. The healing power is the love of the participants and the awesome power of the Holy Spirit healing broken people. The only qualification for attendance is to be a friend or family member of an alcoholic or addict. The meetings are completely confidential and no one is allowed to offer advice.

Lessons Learned

Ironically I encouraged the church I served to invite four Alcoholic Anonymous groups and one Al Anon group to meet at the church many years before I ever attended a meeting. The leader of the AA groups became a friend and confidant over the years and we talked frequently about my struggle in dealing with an alcoholic. He invited me numerous times to attend a meeting of Al Anon at the church. I was not interested in attending a meeting, where there were members of the church I served, and reveal my situation. I was too invested in portraying myself as the competent pastor who had a happy private life. I thought I had everyone convinced that I had my act together. After my first wife divorced me I found out that a number of people were not deceived by my hypocrisy! How pathetic when one tries to project an image that is false. Looking back, I can see this is part of the tension of being a pastor. Churches often have an expectation that their pastor will be a flawless person, and too often we pastors want to live up to that unrealistic false image! Does one lose authority and respect when one admits one's weaknesses? There must be a balance between being completely transparent and having boundaries that maintain a professional relationship. My friend, the Catholic priest Rev Jim Willig was very transparent; but I know he never discussed with his parishioners things that he shared with me. I know nothing about the personal life of my doctor and would not dream of inquiring into a

Lessons Learned

doctor's personal life. So I am not clear about where a pastor should draw the line.

Since I have been divorced and remarried, it has made me more understanding of divorced people. My wife, Marcia, is a Christian and that has been the basis of our relationship even before we dated. The experience of being unevenly yoked in my previous marriage – and now being evenly yoked – has convinced me that there is no comparison between the two different situations. The more I live and breathe the Christian faith, the less interested I am in entertaining differences in basic beliefs. When I first began sharing my near death experience, I hoped to draw atheists, agnostics, new agers, and others into a belief in Jesus Christ. I desperately wanted to be as inclusive as possible and offend no one. The story was always unchanged, but the question-and-answer conversations have changed. What I believe now and what I believed in 1985 has not changed. The difference is: I am more convinced than ever that Jesus is God and Christianity is the way, the truth, and the life! I am less interested in affirming people in their denial of the importance of a relationship with Jesus Christ, and I am becoming bolder in saying so. What is considered to be the traditional Christian faith is my faith, and I am not interested in supporting any other belief system.

Lessons Learned

The people who have had near death experiences are free to interpret them any way they choose. I have been impressed with the testimony of many near death experiencers, and I have been horrified by a few. It is not my responsibility to critique other experiences and I have tried to not be critical. Without being specific, I find some experiences credible and others not credible. I understand the difficulty of trying to speak about the ineffable. It is irrational to put into language experiences that language is incapable of describing. It is like trying to define love. It has never been done, but we keep trying to describe it. Early on I was being interviewed by a newspaper reporter about my experience and he didn't understand what I was saying about the love of God. Out of frustration with him, I said, "God's love is more powerful than an orgasm". He printed that, and I deeply regretted saying that. The statement is true, but it is a vulgar comparison that should not be made out of respect for God. It can be very frustrating trying to speak about things that we are ill-equipped to discuss.

Another danger in having had a near death experience is ego inflation. Any person who is in a position of authority is in danger of feelings of superiority. Having had a major experience of the divine could be the biggest ego inflator of all times. What is better than a direct connection to the Supreme Being? It doesn't get any better than that. There

Lessons Learned

are persons who have had near death experiences who act holier than thou. There are even a few who have exploited their experience to take advantage of people. This makes me doubt everything about them, because if they'd truly had an experience of the divine they would be scrupulous about living a moral life. I have to wonder what they really experienced.

Jesus said to his disciples, "Occasions for stumbling are bound to come, but woe to anyone by whom they come! It would be better for you if a millstone were hung around your neck and you were thrown into the sea than for you to cause one of these little ones to stumble." I take this very seriously, and pray I have never been a stumbling block to faith in Jesus. My intention has always been to accurately describe my experience as honestly as possible and hope that it is pleasing to God that I have done so. Whether people call me a nut case, a fundamentalist, a new ager, a zealot, or whatever; it is their business. I am speaking the truth about God before God, and that is who will judge me. I have been called many unflattering things and it is unpleasant to be trashed. It would be naive to believe that we are all seeking God, and that all people respect others' experiences of God.

One of my pleasures in life is to discuss theology with rational people. I find joy and stimulation in constructive, passionate discussions about God and the Bible. I refuse

Lessons Learned

to discuss God with anyone who is convinced they have the only truth and everyone else is wrong. One of the beautiful ways that God has spoken to me is through people who have different and often greater understandings of theological issues and biblical interpretation. I have belonged to Bible study groups and theological study groups continuously since 1985, and they are one of the joys of my life. It has been a constant source of the Holy Spirit showing up and bringing more light to my limited wisdom. God offers us ways to know and grow in our understanding and intimacy with God. Study of Holy Scripture, participation in the church, and prayer are most important and critical to our spiritual life.

There is no contradiction between my near death experience and my love and involvement in the Christian church. My life as an ordained minister in the church is my testimony about my near death experience. The opportunity to preach from the Bible is an extension of what Jesus taught me on June 1, 1985. It has been a privilege to be part of the Body of Christ, and to laugh and cry, hope and despair, rejoice and grieve with my brothers and sisters in Christ. I hope with all my soul that everyone would be so fortunate to know Jesus as millions of followers of Jesus know Him!

Lessons Learned

1. Every follower of Christ has a testimony about God's work in their lives. These testimonies are important to share because they encourage and offer direction to other Christians.
2. It took fourteen years before I was given a sign by God to write a book about my near death experience. We need to wait upon God to lead us to what we need to do to serve Christ Jesus.
3. God gives us ministries we never imagine are awaiting us. I have a large ministry on the internet that has helped countless people receive Jesus and join the Christian Church.
4. Near death experiences can be a tool to help people find meaning in their lives. NDEs can also be contrary to faith in Christ. We are always free to use and abuse the gifts we have been given.
5. It is essential that we seek and maintain opportunities to study and have fellowship with other Christians. The church is where we typically find brothers and sisters in the Spirit of Christ.

Chapter 11 – Forget About It

Christianity is all about forgiveness. My near death experience was my birthday when I became a child of God. Part of what made that new life possible was being forgiven by Jesus for all of my sins. Jesus and the angels showed me all of my sins and made it known to me that they and God hated my sins, but I was forgiven because I hated my sin as well. Many near death experiences tell of a life review, so I would anticipate that people going to heaven are going to have a life review. Based on my experience and what I have learned from others, those going to hell do not have a life review. God's grace gives the redeemed the opportunity to be forgiven and to be reborn during this life and beyond this life. Christians know the meaning of Easter both in the cosmic consequences and in their personal lives.

Looking back at my life I despise the wrong things that I did. Even the good memories are spoiled by the knowledge of how I failed to acknowledge God. Before I go any further, it is necessary to define sin. Sin is opposing God intentionally. I was a man who thought he was an atheist; everything that I did was shaped by my opposition to God. Even when I did no harm and tried to be a "good" person, it was not with the intention of glorifying God. Without the intention of serving God, there is no good!

Lessons Learned

Every action is based in human depravity without God. For example, caring for your family is elementary and even the animals have some degree of caring for their mate and offspring! Does that make you a good person because you are emotionally attached to your family? Raising a family without God is pure evil. I can't begin to pretend I was a good father because I did not respect God or give my wife and children any appreciation of God. When I was converted my children were teenagers and wanted no part of my new understanding. My wife rejected me and all that I now represented.

Only by the grace, love and forgiveness of God is it possible to live without quilt and shame. I am ashamed for what I have done, but I live forgiven by God, and my Savior died on the cross to win my forgiveness. It would be an even greater sin to deny His sacrifice by denying His victory over sin and death. After my experience with Jesus, I wanted to live a life pleasing to God and that means living the joy that Jesus gives us. "May my joy be in you", Jesus said "and may your joy be complete." That is only possible by being forgiven of our sins. It's important to acknowledge our sins and to ask God to forgive us. When we sincerely repent we are forgiven.

When you put your trust, hope and life in Jesus you do not live in fear of hell. I was given the opportunity to experience hell to a small degree. What happened to me

Lessons Learned

there is more horrible than anyone can imagine. I do not want anyone to think they can avoid hell by empty words or promises. What draws us to heaven is the love of God. The love God gives needs to be returned to the best of our ability. God's love is vast and our love is puny, but it is all God asks of us. I think of Jesus hanging on the cross with His arms outstretched, embracing the whole world with God's love, as he suffered the worst death the Roman Empire had devised. Jesus took upon Himself the sins of the world so that we would be free of the consequence of our sin. To reject Jesus is to reject God's ultimate act of love. We live in a culture that avoids suffering at any cost. How many of us live in a drug and alcohol induced haze to mask suffering? Why are we taking down the images of a suffering Christ on a cross and even eliminating the cross from some of our churches? Jesus' suffering is our salvation! It enrages me that we so cruelly killed Him, but I know it had to be done. Our suffering is so insignificant compared to His suffering. He took upon Himself our sin to give us new life.

Eternal life begins the moment we accept Jesus as the Lord of our life. We are reborn into a completely new life. That is what I experienced, and hope and pray for everyone. It can never be understood until it is experienced. So many people have asked me how they can experience the love of God that I speak about all the

Lessons Learned

time. I tell them to ask Jesus for that love and they will have it. Knowing Jesus as a real person and as the Son of God is the foundation of my life and everything else is based on that foundation. I live in this world, but I am not of this world. I am a visitor, a sojourner, participating in this drama, but it is not who I truly am. My home is in heaven, not here. My heart is in heaven, not here. My hope is in heaven, not here. My greatest love is in heaven, not here. I belong to Jesus and only Him!

Jesus knows everything I have ever done and every thought I have had, and he loves me! He wants you and me to be the persons he created us to be from the beginning of time, and he has done what is necessary for us to be free of our sins. The least I can do is to take Him seriously. There is only one rule, and that is the rule of love. There is only one truth and that is the truth of God's love. Everything else is negotiable. Why do we resist Him? Why is it so hard for people to surrender their delusions of grandeur so they can receive Him? I wish I had the answer to these questions, but I don't have the answers. If I were God, I would make everyone believe somehow, but that is not love. God does not coerce or control us because that would annihilate our free will. God wants us to freely make the right choice. Every minute of every day we have choices to make. Those choices either are more pleasing to God or less pleasing to God. We are

Lessons Learned

responsible for the choices we make. If we try to please God to the best of our ability, we are candidates for resurrection from death to live in our heavenly home. If we fail to do this, we will live far apart from the love of God because that is what we chose. Everyone gets precisely what they deserve. God is not deceived.

God's justice is perfect and it is unlike what we think of as the legal system. God knows the human heart, of which we have no knowledge. Humans judge by appearances, which may or may not reflect the heart of a person. Jesus made me aware of what a hypocrite I had been in my life. I fooled many people with my pretense of being a nice person, but God was not fooled for a second. Jesus hates hypocrisy and expresses his disgust for fakers in many places in the Bible. Perhaps the statement which Christians should pay particular attention to is in Matthew 25:31-46. This is where Jesus condemns counterfeit Christians to damnation. We are not saved by our works, but our lives as followers of Christ must reflect the love of Christ Jesus to the best of our ability. To neglect the great commandment to love one another is to deny Jesus. What is even a greater sin is to do evil in the name of God. The pastors who have sexually used others, the churches that have sought riches and neglected the poor, the teachers of hatred and fear, and the promoters of strife that divide the Body of Christ are the embodiment of damnation.

Lessons Learned

Jesus said there is a sin that is unforgivable. What could that possibly be? Jesus told us we must be prepared to forgive, innumerable times. How then can God be limited in forgiveness, we might wonder. My understanding of the Gospel of Matthew 12:31 is that when we sin against the Holy Spirit we have committed the sin that will not be forgiven. The Holy Spirit is the Spirit of God, the Spirit of Truth, and the Spirit of Christ. The Holy Spirit is the Spirit that resides in us when we receive Jesus as our Savior. To do evil in the name of God is the unforgivable sin. When a person has the Spirit of Jesus in their heart and deliberately opposes that Spirit, they are beyond redemption. How can such a person repent? They have no discernment between what is holy and what is a lie. "You cannot serve two masters", Jesus said. When a person serves the evil one and masks that in Christian guise, they have lost any possibility of salvation because they are incapable of true contrition which is the source of forgiveness. God cannot be deceived, and God's justice is absolute.

God can do anything. God can, for instance, make diamonds out of coal. It is blasphemy to even suggest God is limited in any way. We humans are limited in every way. The knowledge, wisdom, faith, love, and hope we receive from God are precious gifts which must be used carefully. Everything good in life is a gift from God. When

Lessons Learned

God gives us a gift we are expected to use the gift wisely and serve God's purposes with those gifts. What do think of someone who squanders a precious gift? What do you think of someone who perversely uses a precious gift in opposition to the giver of the gift? In in the parable of the talents in Mathew 25:14-30, Jesus warns us about how we must not neglect the gifts we have been given. Our faith in God through the revelation of God in Jesus Christ is the greatest gift any human could receive. It is far more worthwhile than winning the lottery or being elected president of the United States. This treasure beyond any other has to be the focal point of our lives. It is not given for our casual use and it is not given for our worldly benefit. On the contrary the gift of faith and salvation will be costly. When Jesus told us to take up our cross and follow Him, he was giving us fair warning of the cost of discipleship.

When I lost all of my friends after my conversion to Christianity in 1985, I complained to God bitterly about being friendless. God told me I would have new friends and more than I would even know. This was not easy to accept because I was feeling sorry for myself and missed my old friends, such as they were. To this day I miss them, but they have maintained their indifference or antipathy to me. When my wife and children left me I complained in anguish to God, and God answered me. God said I would

Lessons Learned

have a new wife and a new family. God fulfilled that promise as well. When I asked God how he expected me to build a church in Belize without any money, the money came in days after I prayed. God knows we have to let go of certain things in order for new things to happen.

When I talked to Jesus about returning to this world during my near death experience, I asked Him if I would suffer when I came back. He said I would suffer and that this would be an important part of my growth. He kept to His word on both accounts. I suffered physical pain for many months. I refused to take pain medication because I detested what it did to my clarity of mind. The drugs made it impossible to pray and to think about God. I was sick enough without being doped up. I didn't enjoy the pain, but I did learn to cope with it and learned to control it with prayer. With the help of God I could make the pain subside and even dissipate for a while. The frightening part of my illness was losing my strength and eyesight. Eventually my eyesight returned except that I developed cataracts in both eyes that had to be removed and replaced with implanted lenses. My physical strength which had been a major source of pride never came back. I have less than half of the strength that I had before the illness. This has been a blessing because I now cannot intimidate anyone; nor do I have the desire to do so.

Lessons Learned

When we are humbled we do not appreciate it. It isn't in our nature to rejoice in humiliation. Anger and resentment are the first response to getting knocked down. I find myself taking those feelings to God. It is not pretty, but God is big enough to deal with my human weakness. Out of prayer comes resignation which leads to acceptance. From that I can find contrition which is the doorway to forgiveness. From knowing repentance, one can discover a renaissance into something better.

This process has to run its course. My second wife, Marcia, is a long distance runner and she tells me she hates the first three miles and from there it gets pleasurable. I wouldn't know that because I've never run three miles, but this is what she tells me. I have experienced loss and suffering and it does get better after the first three miles or so. Romans 8:28 is a scripture that I have tattooed on inside of my eyelids. It is true, and I have to remind myself of it frequently. It is so powerful that it must be used judiciously. When a person is in the midst of suffering, they are not ready to hear it, but it is available when they are ready. In Romans 5:3-5, Paul writes about how suffering produces character, which produces hope. This process can be rapid or slow. Much of it depends on how much we are introspective and willing to crawl through the mire of self-analysis. There are many shadows in our past that do not invite

Lessons Learned

examination and that prevent the light of truth and God's love from freeing us from the voices of the past.

One way of describing the obstacles to our healing and approach to God are thinking of these barriers as demonic spirits. The voice that tells us we are unforgiveable is demonic. It may have been something implanted in us when we were a child or it is a voice we accepted from a spouse or teacher. This voice is preventing us from approaching God with an open heart and seeking God's forgiveness. This voice is a spirit that controls us and keeps us in oppression.

We allow this voice to have power over our life. It can only be eliminated by recognizing it for what it is and casting it out in the name of Jesus. Depending on how hidden and enmeshed in our being it is, it can be a struggle to free ourselves from its grasp over us. The demonic can only retain its power as long as it is hidden and maintains the illusion of being formidable. This is the deception that gives it security while indwelling inside us. A friend of mind told me he had a monster inside of him that, if ever unleashed, would destroy him. This is the lie that keeps the demon from being discovered for what it is. They are all liars. They only have the power that we give them. When we identify them and confront them with the power of Jesus, the Son of God, they flee from us. The power of evil is no match against the power of

Lessons Learned

God. The power of evil is only the power we give it. God wants us to be free of demonic spirits and will heal us of them if we want to be free.

After we have cast out those demonic influences, we must fill ourselves with more of the Holy Spirit so the demonic cannot return. The evil one knows many tricks, including making a hasty retreat only to sneak back later when we are unaware. A commitment to reading the Bible, attending worship, prayer, and Christian companionship keeps us fortified to live the love, joy and freedom God wants us to know. No matter what our circumstances in life are, God wants us to be fully alive and growing in holiness, which means living in intimate relationship with God as he approaches us in the person of Jesus the Christ. If you want to please God, let God be your God and help you live the life God has given you.

When I was boy, I was enchanted with knights in shining armor. I made mighty swords out of scraps of lumber and armor out of cardboard covered with aluminum foil. For a short while in the fourth grade my group of boys formed the knights of the roundtable. We played in our costumes and had great battles. I collected little cast metal figures of knights and played with them. I read years later what Paul wrote in Ephesians 6:10-17, to put on the full armor of God, and then proceeded to describe in detail what that means. The "armor of God" resonated with me. Saint

Lessons Learned

Paul is so loveable because he speaks as a man struggling in a hostile world to become like Christ using language that we can understand. He doesn't hold back any of his humanity, and that makes him relatable. He is arguably the greatest Christian who ever lived.

Paul tells us "our struggle is not against enemies of blood and flesh," but rather we are up "against the wiles of the devil." When you hear you are fighting demons, don't scoff; if you do, they have already won the battle with you. We are at war with "the forces of evil." Paul repeats the command to "put on the whole armor of God." The following description of that armor relates to what a Roman soldier wore. Keep in mind this was the greatest army the world had known to that time, and the Empire they conquered stood for a thousand years. So, brothers and sisters, why would you not take Paul's commandment to heart? I want to be perfectly clear: I live by this and it has kept me safe from the evil one who hates me with a pure hate and has tried to kill me and defeat me numerous times and in numerous ways. I pray that you will follow Paul in his inspired words to us.

First, we are to "put on the belt of truth." We wrap our abdomen in the truth of Jesus Christ who is the salvation for the world and our personal savior. This is the food which we eat in taking Holy Communion. This is our spiritual sustenance. Second, we are to "put on the

Lessons Learned

breastplate of righteousness." This is obedience to the word of God. It is the righteousness of God into which we are to live; it is not some imagined righteousness of our own. We do nothing apart from the behavior God expects of us to the best of our ability and understanding. Third, onto our feet we "put on whatever will make us ready to proclaim the gospel of peace." We are to be the peacemakers of the world and have no craving for war or division. Fourth, we are to "take the shield of faith which will be able to quench all the flaming arrows of the evil one." Your faith can defeat and defend against anything this wicked world throws at you. There is nothing you need fear from the enemy. Fifth, we are to "take the helmet of salvation." This is the security and knowledge that, as those belonging to Jesus Christ, we will never be lost. And lastly, we are to take "the sword of the Spirit, which is the word of God." We have a weapon to use against the evil one who is the father of lies, and that is the Bible. Paul gives us all the insight we need to be well equipped to be victorious in this world.

It is not a game! We are no longer children. We are striving to save our souls, and the souls of our families, our neighbors and the world. If you do not feel a passion for the eternal security of others, you must already be dead and just don't know it yet. "God so loved the world

Lessons Learned

that he gave His only Son" ... What are you willing to give in order to help save a soul?

Lessons Learned

1. The beginning of our relationship with God is to acknowledge our sin and ask for forgiveness. Jesus has forgiven our sins and wants us to believe in his self-sacrifice for our forgiveness.
2. Life with Jesus Christ is knowing the love of God in everyday life. The greatest gift God gives us is faith, but we have to ask for faith in order to receive it.
3. Following Jesus and loving Him does not mean we will have a carefree life. Even suffering of every kind can be an opportunity to increase our trust in God.
4. We will battle demonic influences in our Christian life. Oftentimes these are "voices" that were implanted in our past and they attempt to be a barrier in our relationship with God.
5. Saint Paul gives excellent guidance in how we can protect ourselves and defeat the forces that want to defeat us in Ephesians Chapter 6.

Lessons Learned

Chapter 12 – My First Church

In the third year of my seminary training I was required to serve a church as student pastor. It was the responsibility of the association minister to place me in that position. That summer I went to Washington DC for a class in a transcultural experience. I was in a group of fellow students at a wonderful church called Church of the Savior. Each of us had been assigned different related missions to work at during the day and in the evening we had a class discussion. I had chosen to work for Manna, an organization which bought dilapidated buildings, renovated them, and then sold them to the poor. I was told I would be doing carpentry so I had brought two large bags of woodworking tools which had been well used when I built my house. The neighborhood to which I was assigned is called Anacostia and was over an hour ride by bus across the city from the house where we were staying near the church building. I was excited about two weeks of being a carpenter, which is something I enjoy.

When I arrived at the jobsite, the man in charge told me I would not need the tools I brought because he needed me to do demolition. The only tools I needed were a wrecking bar and a reciprocating saw which he handed me. The apartment buildings were two story structures build during World War II to house government workers.

Lessons Learned

My job was to remove the steam radiators and the connecting pipes so they could be sold as scrap. So for two weeks I cut and hauled old iron pipes as I removed them from the walls and floors. This was in the middle of the summer and the temperature was in the nineties every day. At the end of the day I would take a shower fully clothed with a garden hose because I was covered in dark soot from the old building. At four thirty I would climb on the bus for the long ride back to the city. I sat alone and people looked at me with disgust because I was still filthy and soaking wet. I was always the only white person on the bus and felt not much appreciated. I didn't blame them, but there was not much I could do working in a gutted building with no facilities.

In the evening we talked about the day's experiences. I had little to contribute because there isn't much to tell about cutting pipes. The other people were working with agencies that dealt with homeless people, AIDS victims, soup kitchens, and other such humanitarian situations. They all had human interest stories to tell. I was alone at my job site and had no such stories to tell. It was just me and the pipes.

At the end of our discussion, we would share prayer concerns and pray together. My one concern was being placed in a church as a student pastor, and every evening we all prayed that God would place me in a church in

Lessons Learned

Cincinnati. Close to the end of my two weeks in Washington, the association minister called and said he had a church that needed a supply pastor for a few weeks and that I should call that church and make an appointment to speak with them when I got home. I was glad to have something, but I thought this was not what I needed. I needed a student pastor position and this was a few weeks supply-preaching. Also, the city of Norwood, where this church was located, had a reputation as a redneck center of bigotry in Cincinnati. I was concerned that the people of the church would fit the stereotype.

When I got home, I made an appointment to meet with a committee of the church to interview with them. When I got there and pulled into the parking lot, I knew I was going to be at this church for a long time, but I didn't know why I felt that. I found out later that the committee members saw me pull in, get out of my car, and agreed they had found their pastor. (This is not the way these things usually happen.) The meeting went well and they told me they wanted me to be their student pastor for at least a year. I asked if they would show me the church which I had never seen and they took me into the sanctuary.

I asked them if I could have some time alone in the sanctuary. They left me there and I went up to the pulpit and said out loud to God, "If you want me here I will do

Lessons Learned

my best; but this is a dying church in a dying town and it is not what I had in mind."

God literally spoke to me, "This is where you are needed."

"If that is what you want," I replied.

That was the end of that conversation. I told the committee I would be happy to be their student pastor, and I needed to know what the salary would be. They told me they could pay me six hundred dollars a month, without any benefits. I readily agreed and signed a contract. I had just taken a one year leave of absence from the university without pay. I had agreed to a salary that was one tenth of what I was making at the university, and without benefits. This was the end of paid health care, big university contributions to my pension, and the probable end of a tenured position that I had worked hard to get. I anticipated my wife was going to be very angry, and she was. Her career as an attorney was taking off and she was making serious money. She never forgave me for leaving the university and becoming a pastor. From her point of view, I was throwing away everything we had worked for to follow a delusion.

There were times when I questioned my sanity. The worship attendance was around fifty and we met in a Sanctuary that seated over three hundred! They had been without a pastor for over two years. Four candidates had

Lessons Learned

turned down their offer. The previous pastor had been forced to leave and there was plenty of leftover anger in the congregation. The physical buildings had been neglected for decades as the congregation dwindled. The roofs leaked, the floors were filthy, and many of the light bulbs were burnt out. The wind blew through the seams in the dilapidated windows. The restrooms were an embarrassment. The carpets were stained. The buildings needed fresh paint inside and out. It was evident the congregation was barely surviving and preparing for the end. The church had had over three hundred people at worship in the early nineteen-sixties and no one had a clue about why they had declined so much in so few decades.

As I sat in my bleak office in the old broken chair at my desk, I asked God, "Where do I begin?" I did not go into the ministry to preside at what seemed to be an extended funeral service.

There was a small bouquet of dusty artificial flowers on the altar. "How long they had been there?" I asked one of the women.

"I don't remember how long they had been there" she answered.

"We need to show our love of God," I suggested "by having fresh flowers on the altar every Sunday."

Lessons Learned

"There is no money to buy flowers" she replied.

"That will not be a problem. God will provide the flowers" I responded. I asked the members of the church if they would like to sign up for the privilege of having flowers on the altar, and there was a signup sheet posted in the hallway to reserve a Sunday. We never had artificial flowers on the altar after that. In fact, sometimes we had so many bouquets we had to think up places to put all of them!

This is not rocket science. The congregation had become passive and despondent. What was killing this church was a lack of enthusiasm for the worship of God.

Soon after putting fresh flowers on the altar, a member of the church came to me and said he had just retired as the head of maintenance for a major Cincinnati company and he would like to help improve the church. Together, he and I stripped and waxed all the floors. He organized groups for painting all the interior rooms and hallways. Over the next few years we renovated the restrooms, replaced all the roofs, landscaped the property, and replaced carpets. The burnt-out light bulbs were replaced, and they shined on a clean and pleasant interior. Spending money on the property was not what anyone wanted to do, but what visitor would return to a shabby, ill-kept church facility?

Lessons Learned

The buildings of the church were mostly empty and this seemed like a terrible neglect of our resources. So I set about seeking appropriate organizations that needed a home or a meeting place. The first group I found to meet in the church building was Alcoholics Anonymous. The question immediately arose about how much income we could make renting space. This was one of my first battles – trying to convince people we were not renting space, and any organization would be considered a guest that could contribute on a voluntary basis.

One of the many lessons I learned in church is the royal use of "we." Some people in the church make their complaints in the plural. For example they would say, "We don't like that hymn", or "we don't like that kind of music". What they are saying is "I don't like it", but it has more force when it is a generalized and universalized statement of displeasure. The church is a place of family dynamics and people use techniques that may work in their family to get their way. Sadly this leads to far too much dysfunctional behavior that has the power to kill a church. It is hard to identify and diffuse dysfunctional behavior. It seems like everyone in the church desperately wants to avoid confrontation and get along, and so they are tolerant of everything. A few people found me non-compliant enough to leave the church, but our average

Lessons Learned

Sunday worship attendance grew to one hundred and fifty over several years.

After a few months the church council offered me the position of pastor. I told them I couldn't accept because I hadn't finished my seminary training and was not yet ordained. They asked if I would accept when I finished my seminary education and was ordained. I agreed and ended up serving that church for fourteen years and left it in good condition.

One of the many mistakes I made at that church was trying to do too much. I worked as many hours as I could. When I finished seminary, I was putting in seventy hours a week and more. There was never enough time to do all the things that I believed just had to be done. There was always someone who needed to be visited and a committee meeting to attend. Sermon preparation, Bible study, Vacation Bible School, food pantry supplies, ministerial responsibilities, weddings, funerals, and on and on, came to occupy all of my life. My home life was miserable so it was more gratifying to work at the church than going home. My wife and children were hostile to what I was doing and I was increasingly indifferent to them. This was a prescription for marital disaster, but I was too busy serving God to see it. My wife was totally engaged in her successful career as an attorney and she worked all the time. She found her own solutions to stress

Lessons Learned

and depression. Over the years she became a completely different person from the one that I had married. We were moving in opposite directions.

I loved my wife, and knew that I was losing her. She refused to go to marriage counseling and was hostile to any suggestion that she had any problems. Our conversations became less frequent and there was increasing acrimony. The worse the situation became, the more we avoided each other to prevent conflict. She found her professional colleagues more gratifying than me. We tried to keep the pretense of civility in public, but it was not very convincing. I was hurt and shamed by her behavior in social situations. She had no reservations about disparaging me in front of our children. Most of her law practice was initially divorces, and she had a strong reputation as a divorce attorney. It never occurred to me that she was methodically preparing for a divorce and she excelled at setting the conditions for her departure.

When I returned home from a mission trip to the Amazon River serving a medical group as evangelist to the people we visited, I returned to an almost empty house, closed bank account, a note from her on the dining room table, and an estranged son and daughter. Within four months we were officially divorced. It was one of the most horrible experiences of my life. I was foolish enough to

Lessons Learned

believe I could convince her to give the marriage another chance. She was not interested.

Thankfully, this took place during a time when I was between churches. I could not have ministered to anyone at this time. For a period of time I sank into a deep depression. I told myself that I was a complete failure because my family had rejected me. Depression deceives us, and we can slip into isolation as the solution to our despair. I didn't want to talk with people or leave the house. My only companion was my dog. She kept me going because she needed me and I needed her. God can even use our pets to keep us giving and receiving love. Without my sweet dog I may have done something regrettable.

Over time, with the help of daily Al Anon meetings, I climbed out of the abyss that had nearly consumed me. Once again God allowed me to be humbled. Looking back on that time, I am thankful for being given the opportunity to descend to the depths of human existence. In hindsight, I have grown more from the hard times than from the good times. I felt no gratitude when I was down; rather anger and despair were my constant companions. How is it possible to grow without struggle? God allows us to fall as far as we need to go and God provides us the means to reach new heights when we are ready. "All

Lessons Learned

things work for God's good purpose for those who love God" according to St. Paul in Romans 8:28.

The church is a jealous mistress and I was easily seduced by her charms. All people are looking for love, and people who go into the ministry are often very needy people. The more I was loved by my congregation, the more love I sought. This is a relationship that is destined to fail because there can never be enough love for an insatiable lover. When my love was spurned by a member of my church, I was emotionally devastated. I took everything personally. When a member of the church died or left for a nursing home, I grieved the loss like a family member. I had no emotional detachment from the congregation. This is not healthy for either party, but I was caught in my own dysfunction. The members of the church knew I loved them, but did they know I loved them too much? I have come to understand that I was enmeshed in inappropriate love, as a pastor with a codependent relationship with the church. On some intellectual level I had insight about what we were doing, but on an emotional level I was totally hooked.

Isn't it intriguing how difficult it is to change one's behavior? How often I have known something was wrong, but continued to keep doing what wasn't working as if there was no other course of action! That is why it is so important that we seek the guidance of good people

Lessons Learned

because they can speak to us through the inspiration of the Holy Spirit and help us make a course correction. If we choose to deceive people or refuse to listen, we will get nothing from others. I find I only want to pay careful attention to Christians because I presume we share mostly the same values. I would not ask an electrician about a solution to a plumbing problem. Nor would I trust a person who did not share my faith in order to help me with a spiritual dilemma. We go to the dentist for dental solutions. My ultimate source of help is God, and I need to know where I have gone off the path and how to get back on it in order to receive God's grace. There is nothing too small or too big that God cannot help us with. The more I live, the more I have become dependent on God's grace. The myth of our culture is that we are supposed to mature into complete self-reliance and security. I have found the opposite to be true. As I mature as a Christian, I am increasingly poor and needy as a spiritual being. Thankfully, God has many brothers and sister in Christ who can listen and speak God's words to us; and thank God for prayer!

A prayer that I repeat frequently is the Jesus prayer. While it has several variations, the version that works best for me is, "Jesus Christ, Son of God, have mercy upon me; for I am a sinner redeemed by your love". I highly recommend this prayer as the beginning of prayer. When

Lessons Learned

it's necessary to find help in prayer, we can consult a source of one hundred and fifty wonderful prayers in the Book of Psalms. If you don't know what to pray, you might look at Psalm 51, and it will speak to you if you have ears to hear. It begins, "Have mercy on me, O God, according to your steadfast love." That is what we are talking about.

Lessons Learned

Lessons Learned

1. Preparation for ministry includes profound experiences in humbling service. God has a plan and a purpose for everything.
2. My first opportunity to serve God's church as pastor was helping the congregation express their love of God. Taking many positive steps to empower the ministry of the members produced a revival in the church.
3. Serving the church as pastor results in many struggles both with some members of the church and with oneself. My church helped me mature as a Christian.
4. Even our weaknesses and failures are important lessons. These learning experiences deepen our faith and ability to follow Christ Jesus.
5. The greatest need we have is for God's grace and the good news is that there is an abundance of grace available to us.

Lessons Learned

Chapter 13 – The Body of Christ

Imagine what the Roman Empire might have been like with today's technology. Rome was brutal and degenerate. Without the influence of the Christian Church, it would not have been a world I would have wanted to live in. Many things we take for granted in our current civilization were actually innovations introduced by Christians. Hospitals, orphanages, public education, universities, and many more are examples of Christian contributions to culture. An example of brutalities no longer a part of life is entertainment by public slaughter of innocent people. We have attempted to build a more just and equitable society with rights for all. Abolition of slavery was a Christian movement, and slavery has been abolished. Slavery was the engine that did the work of the Roman Empire. The contributions of Christianity have unquestionably made the world a much more humane place to live in. Today as the Christian church declines in influence, are we slipping back towards a more brutal world?

The church is the only major institution in our society teaching morality and higher values. The schools don't teach morality, but they do instruct in behaviors to suit

Lessons Learned

their purpose. Our children are too often raised by parents who have little maturity of their own. The church is the light that makes living in our world bearable. If this light is extinguished the world will return to a dog-eat-dog morality. The influence of Christian teachings is taken for granted and even dismissed by secularists. They are ignorant of our history and reckless with our future. Christians espouse a morality that is commanded by God and enforced by a system of justice. Subtract God from the equation and you have a morality dependent on the tyranny of despots like Hitler, leaders of the former Soviet Union, and China's Chairman Mao. The system of justice serves only the whims of the state. That is the alternative to our Christian inspired civilization. As flawed as The United States of America is, would you prefer Nazi Germany as your alternative?

When I began attending church in 1985 it was apparent to me that hope, truth, and a better life were being lifted up every week. This was far different than the cynicism being exalted at the university. The church was the instrument to teach the truth about God, change the world, and bring people to a relationship with Jesus Christ. This was irresistible and I wanted to be a part of it. It became increasingly clear that God was calling me to be a part of the Body of Christ.

Lessons Learned

It is one thing to be enthusiastic about the ideals of the church and quite another matter to help bring them to reality. The church must be more than fine words without substantial actions. My first clue to ministry in the church happened when I was graduating from seminary. We had several special worship services for the graduating seminarians which included guest preachers. Each sermon I heard emphasized the importance of preaching Christ Jesus. This made an indelible impression on me. I have always made the preaching of Christ a major feature of my sermons. This may seem obvious, but be assured Jesus is not always the message in Christian churches. Jesus is the perfect revelation of God and the church is essentially about bringing people to God; therefore we preach what God has revealed. Without the Spirit of Christ being stressed, the Body of Christ is a headless corpse. Jesus is the head, Jesus is the heart, Jesus is the mind, and Jesus is the soul of the church. There must be no other in His place.

In the hundreds of sermons I preached over the decades, no one ever complained about Jesus being raised up in the sermons. The response to preaching from the Bible about Jesus was met with real enthusiasm by the congregations I served. Numerous times people said they had been starving before I came and they were longing to hear this kind of preaching. The more I preached Jesus

Lessons Learned

Christ the more confident I became that this was my task every Sunday. I never repeated a sermon and I found the source book of the Bible to be inexhaustible for material to preach about. The Holy Spirit would reveal new truths every week and fire my enthusiasm for preaching.

My sermon preparation began on Mondays by reading the lectionary selection of Scriptures for that week. On Tuesday I attended a sermon study group with other clergy and we would study the scriptures and discuss their meaning. On Wednesday I would pray about the scriptures and read them and meditate on them. Thursday I would research and write my sermon. Friday I would rewrite my sermon and commit it to memory. Saturday I would rehearse it in my mind and make changes. Sunday I preached without notes and would be surprised at what I had said. No matter what I had prepared the Holy Spirit would often amaze me with something unexpected during the sermon. Those unplanned inspirations were always better than what I had prepared. Every time I preached I gave it over to God and trusted in The Holy Spirit to guide me down the path I had prepared. My hope was to take the congregation with me on the adventure of exploring the revelation of the scriptures, and the nature of Jesus.

Leading the worship was participation within a team of worshippers which included everyone in the church. I

Lessons Learned

have had the good fortune of serving with wonderful organists, choir directors, liturgists, choirs, and inspired congregations. Praising God, praying to God, hearing the word of God, expounding on the word, and sharing this with the faithful is exhilarating! Worship transcends time and space and it is often a connection with God that is unlike anything else in this world. Worship gives me life, hope and faith, every week. When I miss Sunday worship I feel the absence all week long. I hate to miss church and my wife and I rarely do. Too often people go to church as spectators expecting to be entertained. They critically judge the performance of the worship leaders on their entertainment value, and rate the show. These people have completely missed the entire purpose of worship. It is not about what you get from it; rather, worship is about what you put into it. You only get out of it what you have invested in it. We have created a mentality of passive participation in television, movies, sports, and entertainment. Worship does not work this way. Worship is only expressed in active participation, and it is not of much value experienced in passivity.

Over the years, so many people have complained that they have never experienced God. To experience God one has to engage God. That can happen when you pour your whole being into worship. One of the most beautiful worship experiences I have been involved with was in

Lessons Learned

Freeport, Bahamas. We went to a Church of England service with perhaps four hundred Bahamians. My wife and I were the only white people in the congregation. This was a high church with a very complex liturgy. The congregation knew the responses by heart and gave every ounce of energy they had during the worship. We followed along in the Book of Common Prayer as best we could. It was an amazing feeling being with these beautiful people who gave God all they had in worship. It was as if they lifted us up and took us into a heavenly realm with them. I wondered if we had slipped into a room full of angels. When Jesus said each of us is to love God with all of our heart, and all of our mind, and all of our soul, he was heard by his Bahamian brothers and sisters. They experienced God in that church!

I have attended many different denominational churches and I love them all. None is better than another; they are just different in style. I am comfortable in the congregational style of worship, the style in which I was raised. Nevertheless, I fully participate in worship in Catholic, Methodist, Assemblies of God, Lutheran, Orthodox, Church of Christ, Baptist, Presbyterian, non-denominational, Full Gospel, Episcopal, Messianic Jewish, or any other Christian group. God loves them all and I do too. Of course, some musicians are better than others, but so what? Some preachers are better than others, and

Lessons Learned

what is your point? Some churches have beautiful stained glass and others have none at all, and who cares? It is not about the show. Yes, I love a good show but that is not what I went to church for; rather, I went to give God glory.

Let me tell you about worship in the poorest church I have ever attended. I was on a mission trip with a large group of Christian medical people. We had doctors, nurses, pharmacists, and aides. I was the sole pastor, and my job was evangelism of the people we served along the Amazon River. I told the gospel to groups of about eight people with a translator, all day long. After I told them the gospel, I asked them if they had accepted Jesus as their Lord and Savior. In every group some said they had and we prayed for them. The remaining people were asked if they would like to receive Jesus as their Lord and Savior. In every group some asked to receive Jesus. We would pray for them and then we would lead them in prayer to receive Jesus Christ. We were visiting villages where few missionaries, if any, had visited. Sixty five people asked to receive Jesus during that week.

On the last day we split the team into two groups because there were separate villages on either side of the river which was close to a mile wide at that place. In the afternoon one of our boats came for me. I was told me to hurry and come across the river because I was needed immediately. I became anxious because I assumed

Lessons Learned

something terrible had happened. When we got to the other side of the Amazon the villagers were waiting for me. They had requested a pastor. When I began the long walk from the riverbank to the village, the villagers cheered my arrival and followed me. When I asked the medical team why they had sent for me, they told me the villagers needed me to pray with them. They invited all of us to come to their church for worship. We walked farther away from the river deep into the jungle. We had no idea what to expect. It was mid-afternoon and we would normally be getting ready to leave the village for the ship we lived on, and yet we were walking deeper into the jungle on a narrow path, accompanied by a couple hundred villagers.

When we got to the church building I saw that it was a thatch roof covering an area the size of a four car garage. Inside were a few planks for sitting; nothing else. I was informed that I would be preaching a sermon. A man brought a homemade conga drum, and another man had a homemade guitar with four strings. They started playing and a few old women came forward and began to sing in Spanish. Then young women and children came forward and began to sing and dance. Soon everybody joined the group in the singing. It was as heartfelt and joyful as if this was the most wonderful day of days. Time went by as if minutes were seconds and hours were minutes. It became

Lessons Learned

dark and we had only a few lanterns to light the space. I preached a complete sermon in Spanish, which is a language I know very little. People came forward for healing and we prayed in teams for them. Cripples were healed, the blind received sight, ears of the deaf were opened, and tumors disappeared. The American doctors were shouting praises to God in utter amazement at seeing miracle after miracle happen before their eyes. We were all crying out of joy. This went on for hours. It was late, it was very dark in the jungle, we were miles from the river, and far from our boat which was our home. When the service was over we processed back along the narrow trail with the villagers. When we got back to the boat we had dinner and talked. None of us had ever experienced anything so powerful before. The doctors and the nurses were more impressed than the rest of us because they witnessed things that cannot happen in modern medicine. Instantaneous healing is quite miraculous. It seems like that worship went on for many hours outside of time. We were in the presence of a people who really had faith in God; and God showed up! God can do anything, and God loves people who love God.

These miracles were witnessed by over thirty American missionaries, many of whom were doctors and nurses, along with the more than one hundred people of the village. These are not the only miracles of healing I have

Lessons Learned

personally witnessed, but my topic is worship and this is to illustrate what can happen in worship. I am aware that there are false healers and charlatans in the Christian healing realm. They by no means detract from the legitimate miracles that happen regularly around the world. Many miracles take place in all churches frequently. Those are the miracles of lives being changed by the gift of faith in Jesus Christ. All the psycho-pharmaceutical drugs and all the psychotherapy that people have cannot compare to the spiritual healings that are taken almost for granted in the Christian church. Lives are radically changed and restored to health by the power of the Spirit of Christ. Many Christians expect this and regard it as normal in the church. I have been aware of this miracle of "resurrection" hundreds of times. Personally, I consider a miracle of spiritual rebirth greater than a physical healing, and much more difficult to effect.

A group from our church went on a three-day retreat to a church camp in central Ohio. We were there with several dozen other members of various churches from around the state. We divided-up into small groups for a program of study and discussion. During one of those times when we were sharing with each other our relationships with God, a particular individual became the concern of the group. She was a woman in her late thirties with three teenage children and a loving husband. The woman told

Lessons Learned

us that she had been active in the church all her life but had never felt God's love or presence. She was deeply upset about her lack of relationship with God because she had been an ardent churchgoer and worker, and felt like she had no real faith because she had never experienced God in any way. Several of us in the group simultaneously urged her to leave us and go into the woods and pray to God, for God to make God's presence known to her. We promised her that we would pray for her and she must persevere in prayer until her prayer was answered. She left us to journey into the woods.

As soon as she was out the door, we began discussing what had happened. All of us agreed it was very risky promising someone an experience of God, and especially promising that to a person that was having a crisis of faith. All of us agreed that we needed to get to work praying in earnest for this woman alone in the woods hoping for a sign from God. Over an hour passed before she returned.

The instant she walked through the door we all quietly began praising God because all of us could see she had a light surrounding her. This light is often a sign of God's presence. This woman's face was radiant with joy. When she approached us we were anxious to have her relate what had happened to her in the woods. She told us she had found a pleasant place to sit by a stream and had prayed as we had instructed her. After a while the rustling

Lessons Learned

of the leaves and branches began the most beautiful music she had ever heard. The sunlight became a white light like she had never seen before, and the light enveloped her. She was filled with a sense of peace she said she could not describe, and then she was overwhelmed with love so powerful she had no words to describe it. At this point in her recounting of her experience she was crying and all of us were crying. Then she said, "I think that was God, don't you?" We all laughed and told her that was definitely God and she had the answer to her prayer and our prayers.

The church has access to a power of which the world is unaware. The people in the Body of Christ have no power of their own, but they can access God who is all powerful. God does not take orders from people and God is going to do things only according to the mysterious ways of God. God's ways are not our ways, and we need to understand that. The church, which is the Body of Christ, was created to be God's instrument for the transformation of humanity. God created humans to be more than animals. We are created to become the true sons and daughters of God, and the church is the only means by which that is possible. If there is no Christian church, there will be no Bible, no knowledge of Jesus Christ, and no plan of salvation for the sinners of the world. Without the Christian church, evil will thrive and overwhelm the

Lessons Learned

remnant of people who have some appreciation of God. I believe that would be cause for God to destroy all humankind and start over with a new creation.

My task is to be a prophet of hope and not doom. The dilemma is that there are too many trends taking place in the world that we live in to be oblivious to the potential for the destruction of humankind. The Christian church is dying in Europe and in the United States. The church is growing in South America, Africa, and Asia. What does this mean for the future? I don't know. What I do know is that The United States has been blessed by God for a purpose and when we betray God we will lose the blessing. The future of the United States is linked to the success of the church in the US. As American Christians become increasing fervent with their personal salvation and holiness, the majority of their fellow Americans are becoming indifferent to God and hostile to the church that Jesus established. The concern for the welfare of the United States is based in love of God and love of this country. Too often it feels like we are a calamity about to happen, and this creates in me a sense of urgency about the need to build up the church for the salvation of the world that I know and love. What more can I say? There is not much time left for the conversion of the United States of America.

Lessons Learned

Lessons Learned

1. The influence of the Christian Church in society is more profound than most people imagine. Civilization would be much different without the contribution of the church.
2. Worship is participation in the joy and the love of God. All worship is good, but we appreciate most the type we are most familiar with.
3. The Holy Spirit is a vital part of the worship experience. There are times when the power of the Holy Spirit does miraculous things in worship when faith is present.
4. Everyone can experience the presence of God in worship and in their lives. The community of the faithful needs to encourage and pray for people to experience God in their lives.
5. The alarming decline in church attendance in the United States will lead to the downfall of this country. We desperately need a national revival.

Chapter 14 – A Promise to Lydia

God speaks to us all the time and the question is whether we are listening or not. God speaks in small still voices.

We had an active clergy group that met monthly, and every year a member of the group, Rev. Tom Eisentrout, would speak about his mission trips to Central America. In 2000 Tom showed slides of his most recent trip to Mexico where they had poured a concrete roof on a church they helped build. Tom asked me if I was interested in going on the next trip in January. This was something he had asked me repeatedly and I had always said I was not interested. This time I was intrigued by the images he showed. Reluctantly, I finally decided to go on a foreign mission trip. Before this I was never convinced this was something I wanted to do, and now I was going.

When we arrived in Belize we were taken by van three hours north to a hotel in Corozal town where we were fed and settled in for the night. The next morning we drove forty-five minutes to a small village at the end of a long, pot-holed road called San Victor. We were dropped off and told that one of the teachers at the school would show us what to do. We had been told we would be helping to build a classroom building for the school and

Lessons Learned

we anticipated that we would be helping to lay concrete blocks. The teacher greeted us and showed us the site of the new school building. The excavation of the ground for the footers had just begun. The building was ninety feet by thirty feet. The footers needed to be dug three feet deep by three feet wide. Only a fraction of the site had been excavated. We were told our job was to complete the digging for the footer. We asked if they had any tools. We were informed that we needed to go around the village and ask to borrow tools from the people. So my son-in-law Addison and I volunteered to attempt to procure the tools. Most of the homes were small one room dwellings made with stick walls and palm thatch roofs in the traditional Mayan style. Many of the houses had only a curtain over the doorway and there was almost no window glass in the village. Most of the homes had no electricity and none had running water or plumbing. Each house had a hand-dug well in the front yard, and an outhouse in the backyard. At times it felt like we were in an ancient Mayan village.

As we walked through the village people disappeared into their homes, and they avoided any contact with us. We asked at every house we came to and a few villagers responded. After an hour or two we had collected a few broken shovels, two pick axes, and an iron bar. We had to make a couple of new handles for the antique tools

Lessons Learned

because some of them were broken. One of us had brought duct tape so we repaired the ones that had cracked wooden handles. We got some stout sticks and made new handles for the ones that we could repair.

The foundation was outlined with strings so we started digging. To our surprise after the first few inches of vegetation and top soil there was a harder layer of subsoil for a few more inches. Under the sub soil was marl, which is limestone that can only be broken with a pickax, a few inches at a time. Swinging the pickax was exhausting so we took turns hammering away at the limestone. There were seven of us missionaries and three were women. The women couldn't handle a pickax so they shoveled. By lunch time we had dug a few feet of foundation. We had no food or drink so the women set off around the village to find a store to buy food. They came back with two loaves of white bread, four cans of spam, bottles of coke, and a jar of pickles. The sandwiches tasted great because we were so hungry. We sat in the shade and feasted. Some of the school children observed us from a distance. After lunch we went back to digging.

That evening we were picked up by the van which returned us to our hotel in town. That evening we thought that with a few more tools we might be able to complete digging the foundation in the five days we had to work there. We had inquired if there was a backhoe we could

Lessons Learned

rent and were told there was no backhoe in this part of Belize (which was not true). The next day we borrowed a few more tools and dug all day. While we were having lunch, some of the school children came closer and we had an opportunity to talk with them. The little children spoke only a few words of English, but the older children spoke English well because Belizean children are required to learn English in school. Some of the boys asked if they could dig with us. We gladly accepted their offer and we made more progress than the day before. We gave the boys a few dollars for helping and they were delighted to receive the American money. We would later find out that we could have hired men from the village for five dollars a day and had the foundation done in two days! After five days, we had completed the digging of the foundation and had made friends with many children. In the evenings we couldn't wait to get into our showers and wash the sweat and dirt off of us. We ate at the hotel and filled ourselves with delicious dinner to be ready for the next day of hard manual work. So, none of us were very pleased with our mission experience.

On the last day in the village, we were getting ready to leave San Victor village, never intending to return; however the children we had befriended surrounded us as we said our goodbye. Two girls Lydia Kau and Ermina Ewan, were holding my hands and holding onto me as the

Lessons Learned

missionaries climbed into the van. Lydia and Ermina were crying, and I asked, "Why are you crying?"

"I will never see you again" said Lydia.

"Lydia," I said, "I will come back next year and see you." I regretted saying this before I finished saying it. I was making a promise to two children and I could not fail them. At that moment I knew I was coming back to San Victor next year.

When I returned to the United States I started talking about forming a group to go to Belize in a year. Everywhere I went I talked about Belize, its wonderful people, and their needs. We had been sent to this village on the recommendation of the Catholic priest, Father Hall, because he said it was the poorest village in the district and needed the most help. The school was his worst school and that is why we were helping to build the school. The Catholic elementary school was the only school in the village. It offered classes from first grade to eighth grade to two hundred students. Only a few students graduated from the eighth grade each year and fewer still went on to the high school located six miles away. The importance of education for improving the lives of the people of Belize was obvious. We were informed the school needed ten thousand dollars more to complete the school, in addition to the three thousand dollars that

Lessons Learned

we gave them. The mission group I formed in the United States soon raised the money and sent it to Father Hall.

This new group of missionaries I recruited returned a year later, the school building had the concrete block walls finished, and the forms were in place to pour the concrete roof. The men of the village had contributed all of the labor. The roof was covered in a grid of steel reinforcing rods, and required thirty cubic yards of concrete to complete it. A friend of mine back in Ohio was a professional concrete contractor, so I explained the situation to him. In Belize we would be mixing the concrete in two small mixers on the ground and hauling the concrete up to and around the roof in one pour. He told me it could not be done in one day and we would have to put a rubber gasket into the seam and plan two days for the complete pour. When I got to Belize with my expensive rubber gasket the Belizeans told me they would do it in one day and we would not need the gasket. I was skeptical, but could not convince them to plan a two-day pour, using a rubber gasket for the seam.

Sunday is the only day the men of the village are not required to work in the cane fields, so we started pouring on Sunday morning at five am. Ninety men showed up to help. Nearby, a group of village women made refreshments for us. The scaffold was constructed of sticks nailed together to position a human chain lifting five

Lessons Learned

gallon buckets of concrete up to the roof from the ground. It looked very fragile. I took a job running a cement mixer. No one took a break from the work and by two o'clock in the afternoon the thirty cubic yards of concrete were poured. During the work there was no yelling and no one gave orders. Every man took a position and seemed to know exactly what to do. Only when the work was completed did the men stop for refreshments. I have never experienced such hard working people who could work so harmoniously without anyone giving instructions. It was an amazing experience for me and the other Americans who worked that day. The rest of that week we built doors and window shutters out of rough-sawn lumber for the new building. The building contains three classrooms which were desperately needed since these classes previously had to meet outdoors because there was no space for them in existing buildings. When it rained, classes were dismissed. Today the building has added two bathrooms on one end and serves the children well.

Today, San Victor Roman Catholic School has over two hundred students. The majority of the students graduate eighth grade – more than twenty children each year. More than half of these children attend the high school in San Narciso village, six miles away. A number of these students have gone on to complete junior college and a

Lessons Learned

few have completed four years of college at the University of Belize. We have been supplying scholarships to pay the tuition at the High Schools. The principal of the San Victor School, Maestro Benito Pantin, told me a few years ago that the school had been named the best school in Belize. I have attended several graduations and I am so proud of the young people who are now prepared to accomplish whatever they choose to do in the world.

It has become abundantly clear to me, over the years working with the people of San Victor, that the cruelest part of abject poverty is how much it limits human potential. In the past, the children of San Victor had no alternative to doing what their parents did to survive. The men cut sugar cane for an average of one thousand dollars a year. This made the men crippled with arthritis in their forties and they died when they were about fifty years old. The women married in their early teens and had as many babies as possible in the hopes that some would survive and help support their parents in their old age, in their forties and fifties. The women worked hard from before sunrise to after dark caring for their families. Many people had only one change of clothing. Things have now changed in the village dramatically but this was the way it was in the beginning of the twenty first century. Life was not very different for the people of San Victor than it had been for their Mayan ancestors for

Lessons Learned

thousands of years. The people of the village are very clean and make the best with very little. Cooking is done outside the home over a wood fire. Washing is done daily with a washboard and a bucket. Most of the children are immaculate.

If an uneducated boy or girl wanted to escape this fate of poverty of their parents and grandparents, he or she ran away to a city. Their fate in the city was almost certain to be catastrophic. The following is the scenario that is played out thousands of times all over the world, and it is absolutely common in Belize. The teenager hops on a bus to a city. When they arrive a well-dressed man befriends them and asks them if they are looking for a job or a place to stay. This friendly person takes them to an apartment and offers them food, clothes, work, and everything that the teenager desires. Too soon this innocent is hooked on drugs and selling himself or herself for sex on the street or pushing drugs. In a few years in the city this beautiful innocent from the village is disease ridden, filthy, and dying with no place to go. They are used-up and thrown out like the trash by their pimps. Some brave missionaries have tried to rescue children in the cities, but it is extremely difficult to save them once they have been hooked on drugs.

The evil one is the father of lies and he preys on the innocent to corrupt and destroy them. We have defeated

Lessons Learned

the evil one's plans for some of the children of San Victor by equipping them with Christian faith and an education that gives them both knowledge and skills to have a productive life. Most of the people in San Victor village are Catholic. There are some other Christian groups in the village and we have given material help to those groups when they asked. The second year I visited in the village, as we were working on the classroom building, I began asking villagers, "what the greatest need of the village?" Everyone I asked told me they needed a Catholic Church. They explained that when the priest came to the village once a month for mass, the Catholics would meet in a school classroom building and have mass there. I attended some of these masses and they were pleasant, but the setting was cumbersome at best with the little tablet chairs in a crowded elementary classroom. The school had religious instruction in the school curriculum, which was wonderful. There was no place for all the students to assemble at one time. If they had a church building, it could be used both for worship, and also used by the school and the community. It was evident that the village would be well served by having a church that would meet many needs.

I talked to the new priest, Father Chris Glauncy, and he told me they would be very pleased to have a church built, but there was no money for it. It would cost twenty-

Lessons Learned

five thousand dollars, in material alone, to build an adequate church. Fr. Chris knew the people of the community would contribute the labor. I told him I would see if we could help in some way, but I had no idea how that would happen. When I returned to the US and my job as a full time pastor in Cincinnati, I was troubled. I didn't' have any idea where I was going to raise twenty-five thousand dollars for a Catholic church in Belize. The church I served was in a declining neighborhood and I was in the process of trying to grow the church attendance and repair the church's property. I prayed to God to show me the way. Days went by without an answer. A few days later a man came to worship on Sunday, and after the service he said he would like to speak with me. When I had finished speaking to everyone else, I went over to him and asked him what he wanted. I assumed he had come seeking assistance. Instead, he said, "I have something for you." He handed me a check. I took it from him and looked at it. It was made out to me in the amount of twenty thousand dollars.

"Is this was a joke?" I asked him. He assured me it was real. Amazed, I asked him who he was and why was he giving me this money. He told me he'd had a dream and God told him to give Howard Storm the money to build a Catholic church in Belize. I asked him why he would do such a thing because of a dream. He said God kept giving

Lessons Learned

him the exact same dream and he knew after a while he would have no peace until he obeyed. He said he had a hard time finding me because he didn't know where to look and he knew nothing about me. He finally called different churches until he found me.

I called Fr. Chris in Belize and told him I would be sending him twenty thousand dollars to construct a new church in San Victor village. I also told him I would be praying for the five thousand dollars needed to complete the church project. He told me he would talk to the villagers and get things started. By the grace of God, that week I received a check in the mail for another five thousand dollars for my mission work in Belize. I called Fr. Chris and told him I would be sending five thousand dollars more, and that apparently, God really wanted this church built. He agreed. Every few weeks I would talk to the priest on the phone and he would give me progress reports. The villagers were very excited about the new church project and pledged their labor to complete the church. That winter I took a group of missionaries to Belize and we had the opportunity to lay some concrete blocks in the walls of the church. The church was being built rapidly with the labor of the people of San Victor voluntarily doing all the work. The consecration of the completed church was scheduled for the late spring and Bishop Martin of Belize was coming to consecrate the church. I was invited to

Lessons Learned

attend the consecration. I was most excited to participate in this ceremony!

There were several hundred people at the consecration and I had the privilege of meeting Bishop Martin. After the consecration he invited me to have lunch with him in one of the classroom buildings which a few village women had prepared. I expected there to be a large crowd at the luncheon and was surprised that it was just for me and the Bishop. He said he wanted to speak with me privately. "When I was first ordained in my early twenties", he began "I was given the parish of Corozal District to minister". That had been fifty years ago and San Victor was a very primitive traditional Mayan village at the time, on many occasions when he had attempted to reach the village, the path through the jungle was impassable by horse and he had to turn back. God had given him a love for the people of the village and he had prayed for fifty years that someday San Victor would have a church." Bishop Martin told me with tears in his eyes that he was retiring this year and the consecration of the Catholic Church in San Victor was the answer to his prayer. He thanked me for what I had done to help make this happen.

I told him that I had done very little and I recounted how the money had come to me after I had asked God to raise the money. He was not surprised by the miraculous

Lessons Learned

account I told him. He thanked me for having the faith to make it possible and I thanked him for the honor of helping God fulfill his prayer and his faith. We both agreed that God wanted this church for this little village and the people would grow in their faith by having the church, and that the school would make good use of the building. It was evident Bishop Martin was a holy person and had a deep love for the people of San Victor.

For the next mission trip we had raised a few thousand additional dollars to buy ceramic tiles to cover the concrete floor along with lumber to build more benches for the people to sit on. The church can seat two hundred and fifty people and is used frequently by the school and the village as well as for weekly worship. The priest who serves the entire district still can only visit the village once a month because he serves a district with over thirty-six thousand people who are mostly Catholics. The people of the village have services there every Sunday and on Holy days. They have communion with elements that have been consecrated by the priest at previous masses. The attendance at mass has increased and the church has grown stronger.

When we go to Belize we have a weeklong Bible school in the church for the children of the village. We always have about two hundred children attending our Bible schools. We are not bringing Christianity to heathens. We are

Lessons Learned

nurturing the Christian faith to people who are in diverse stages of their faith journey. God works in mysterious ways and what a joy it is to be a part of God's way in the world. I will be forever thankful to Lydia and Ermina for caring about me and drawing me back to Belize.

Lessons Learned

Lessons Learned

1. When we are attentive to God's call, we find ourselves blessed in unknown adventures. The fruits of those journeys can develop over years.
2. When we serve God by responding to God's call, there will be an abundance of support for the work to be done.
3. In our mission work we knew we were fighting a battle for the souls of the poor we served. Evil is painfully real to the poor in developing countries.
4. God wants the Christian church to be present in the lives of his beloved people. God will provide a way for the church to be built.
5. Most Americans live lives of affluence and the majority of the world live in relative poverty. We have an obligation to God to help our sisters and brothers around the world in any way we can.

Lessons Learned

Chapter 15 – Loaves and Fish

For the next twelve years I organized mission trips to San Victor. God blessed the people of San Victor with the generosity of thousands of Americans. The majority of the people who supported the mission never went there, and they would never meet the beautiful Maya and Mestizo people that we came to love. The hundreds of people that went on the missions were blessed by the experience, and most especially by the faith of the people who had so little material wealth compared to the Americans, but they were rich in faith. I told the missionaries they got more spiritually from the people than from what we gave them in material goods. Most would agree that their lives were changed by the mission experience. It is amazing how God blesses those who make an effort to please God by extending themselves and doing sacrificial giving. As Jesus said, "It is more blessed to give than to receive."

The Americans were told repeatedly they were on this mission to be instruments of God's love, and they were the ambassadors of Christ to share God's love in practical and spiritual ways. The emphasis was always on building relationships with the people of the village. Many of the Americans fell in love with the Belizeans and built lasting relations with the people of San Victor. God's love is not an abstraction or a theory. The love of Christ is tangible

Lessons Learned

and real, transmitted between people of faith. The examples of how this happened in San Victor would fill books. The following are a few examples of the reality of that love.

On the first mission trip to Belize we organized in 2002, a group of doctors agreed to come and give free medical services to five villages. We made all the necessary arrangements with the Belize medical authorities for the doctors to practice medicine in Belize beforehand with the help of the Catholic priest Fr. Chris Glauncy, who served the northern part of Belize. The doctors had procured contributions of medicine and supplies worth thousands of dollars. They had support staff of several nurses, pharmacists, and intake help. At the village clinics the medical teams examined between one hundred to two hundred people a day. They gave away all their supplies and dealt with a wide range of conditions. Many women brought their children to be examined. Some elderly came with disabling problems. Men and women arrived with every kind of complaint. Most of the people had never been to a doctor. Doctors in Belize are expensive for people who live on a subsistence income. The poor just suffer and endure whatever comes to them. Even if they went to a doctor they knew they can't afford the medicine or treatment prescribed by the doctor. There is no safety net in the developing world.

Lessons Learned

Among those who came was a young man who arrived at one of the clinics with a two-inch metal piece in his arm and it was terribly infected. They questioned him and discovered it had been in his arm for several weeks. He admitted he had been unable to remove it because it was so deep. They improvised a surgical area and removed the metal from his arm and filled him with antibiotics. He was sent away with bottles of antibiotics. He told them he could not afford a doctor so he just tolerated the pain as he cut sugar cane for a living.

The doctors were so impressed by the people they treated and their need for medical attention they organized yearly trips to do medical missions all over Belize and over the years their mission has grown and expanded to surgical teams that do free major surgery in the Belize hospitals. They also do training for health care providers in Belize. Their work has affected the lives of thousands of Belizeans. All of their work is given freely and at considerable sacrifice to the doctors, nurses, dentists, and other health care providers.

One day I was talking with Carmello Kau about the house we were building for him and his family in San Victor when he told me his brother had a sick baby. He asked if I would look at the baby next door. I was introduced to the mother and the newborn baby, Lucy. The tiny baby had a cleft palate that was extreme. The medical team was

Lessons Learned

coming to a nearby village that day and I told the parents I would bring a doctor to look at their baby. I left the village and requested a doctor to come with me to see the baby in San Victor. Dr. Mary Ann Barnes came with me and examined the baby. She told us the upper palate was cleft and exposed the brain. The baby would die soon without major surgery which needed to be done in the United States. Dr. Barnes told us she would make arrangements as soon as she returned home to get the baby and mother to Cincinnati for the necessary surgeries. Within days the mother and child were in Cincinnati and the child had several surgeries to repair her palate and lip. Years later Lucy is a healthy child. They were in Cincinnati for many months and everything was donated. A Methodist church in Ohio gave that family a beautiful new home in San Victor to support that family.

This is one story out of countless examples of lives saved and transformed by Christian love, lived in real time and space. Over the years, I have heard criticism from skeptics about the value of Christian missionaries working in underdeveloped countries. When I look at the lives that have been saved, the children educated, the hopeless given hope, the houses built, and the path to eternal life opened up, it is a joy to have been a missionary. The critics of Christian missionaries are completely ignorant of the good being done all over the world in the name of

Lessons Learned

Christ. If more people supported Christian missions, the world would be a different place.

I remember the day I was walking through the village and came upon a man with whom I had worked mixing concrete for the school roof. He invited me to meet his wife and children. We talked outside his home. His house was typical for the village. It was approximately twelve feet by eighteen feet in dimension. The walls were composed of palmetto palm trunks tied together and arranged vertically. The corners were stout logs which provided the structural stability for the house. The roof was palmetto palm thatch. This design and construction was ancient Mayan design. His home was about ten years old and he had built it when he married. He was a cane cutter and worked six days a week with a machete cutting cane. He was very cheerful and pleasant. His family slept in a hammock and they had three wooden chairs and a table. They cooked behind the house on a wooden fire. His passion in life was soccer and he was part of the village soccer team. As we talked I was aware of this fine young man living in a tiny house with a dirt floor working very hard to feed his family. I knew I needed to do something to help this family. He had no complaints and asked me for nothing. There were over a hundred families just like his in the village.

Lessons Learned

When I returned home I knew that there had to be a way to provide better homes for the people of San Victor. The obvious solution was to use my carpenter skills. I decided to build homes. I made four houses in my back yard out of panels that could be assembled on site. I bought a steel container and packed the houses in the container and had it shipped to San Victor. My friend in Belize had concrete slabs prepared for the four houses beforehand. When our group arrived in San Victor, we assembled the prefabricated the houses in a week and helped the families move in before we left. One of the families we gave a house had twelve children. Another family, a single mother and eight children got a house. This was very gratifying, completing four houses in a week.

Talking with my best friend in the village, Armando Teck, it became evident there was a better way to create housing in the village. We evaluated the need based on the number of children in the family, the work habits and sobriety of the father, willingness to work on other houses, and general character of the family. From that time on we hired Armando and his crew who built the structure and we installed doors, put wooden shutters in the window openings, built interior partitions, and painted. The labor costs were only a small fraction of the total cost because much of the labor was donated from men qualifying for a house in the future, by contributing

Lessons Learned

sweat equity. We built wooden houses for three thousand five hundred dollars and concrete block houses for five thousand dollars. Anyone wanting a concrete house was required to buy their block which cost about four hundred dollars. All the roofs were made of an aluminum alloy which lasts a long time. The concrete block is covered with a coat of stucco and painted inside and out. These houses are generally sixteen feet by twenty feet which is larger than the homes the people were used too. The interior was divided into two or three rooms. In ten years, with the cooperation of many churches we built seventy-three houses in the village of San Victor and many houses in other villages. Using this method, I estimate we built roughly one hundred homes in ten years for four hundred thousand dollars. A single house in the United States could easily cost that much.

In a mission group, the skills and abilities of the group vary widely. Many of the groups that I led were youth groups with very few useful skills, so we did a lot of painting. When we first came to San Victor there were very few painted buildings. The village was all different shades of grey and brown. After ten years the village was a vibrant Caribbean looking mix of pastels. When we had skilled craftsmen, we took advantage of their ability. If we had an electrician, he would spend the week improving the wiring at the school. When a plumber came, we

Lessons Learned

organized the teenagers into work teams and on that trip we installed one hundred and ninety showers for every house in the village. These are showers in the back of the houses with walls for privacy. Prior to the showers the villagers took bucket baths in the yard.

When we first came to San Victor very few houses had electricity. Today every house has some electricity. There was no running water in the village in the early days. The government installed a water system in 2004 with a deep well and a water tower. This water was much cleaner than the shallow wells the people had previously used, and a man in the village is paid to add chlorine to the water tower. This has made the village much healthier. I was told the government installed this water system because of all the attention we had brought to the village. We built a large bathroom and shower facility at the school which then also served the church. A major part of that project was a septic system which included hiring a backhoe to dig the hole for the septic tank. These were the first flush toilets and showers in the village. More people have added flush toilets since that time.

Part of our Christian mission has been to improve the health and hygiene in the village along with education, housing, and faith-building. In the teacher's bathroom at the school there is a framed photograph of me with a caption underneath it. The caption quotes me stating, "I

Lessons Learned

care about you from top to bottom." I am very proud of that tribute and stand by it. Jesus healed people, fed people, taught, and showed them the way of salvation. We have tried to follow the example of Jesus in our mission work and cover all aspects of the human condition.

One of the greatest joys in our work has been the Bible schools we have conducted for the children. Almost all the village children attend our week-long schools. My wife, Marcia, has been the organizer of these schools and they are labor intensive work. Our daughter, Angela, has also been a major contributor to these schools over the years. We teach Bible stories, crafts, music, activities, and offer the ever-popular snacks. Many of the mothers attend the schools and bring their babies. We supplement the religious instruction that is a part of the curriculum of San Victor Roman Catholic School. Along with the outreach to the children we have attempted to evangelize all the adults. We have passed out Bibles to everyone who wanted one. We hold worship services and invited villagers. I spend a good deal of time meeting villagers in their homes for pastoral conversations. We have been blessed on almost every trip with pastors and priests who have visited the homes of the villagers. We are ecumenical in all our work. We have worked with the small Pentecostal church, Seventh Day Adventist church,

Lessons Learned

and the Baptist church in the village. We all get along because we are all Christians and not divided by denominational differences. In the United States there can be real animosity between some denominations, but in the mission work I have usually experienced cooperation.

One mission group of over sixty people was having inspired worship one evening, and the worship leader asked everyone to state what church they belonged to in the United States. We counted fifteen different denominations and two dozen different churches. There has never been a problem in the missions with people squabbling over religious differences. I consider this a miracle of God's grace since this would not be the case back home. Even in one congregation people are too often divisive. It has been a great thrill for me to see people transformed by the Holy Spirit on these trips and become more compassionate and selfless. Of course, we have had a few people who have been nothing but trouble, but they have been the exceptions and I'm glad to say they have never succeeded in ruining the mission experience for the entire group. At times, I have been pushed to the breaking point because of these difficult individuals. When I'm in San Victor, my time and energy is devoted to the concerns of the villagers and the welfare of the missionaries, and the destructive individuals

Lessons Learned

occasionally sap my emotional energy and steal my time to deal with them. It's hard to not deeply resent their intrusion into my focus on what truly is important on these mission trips.

There is a force of evil in the world, and it hates God, Jesus, the Christian Church, and Christian missionaries. This evil is out to defeat our efforts and it works through troublemakers to wreak havoc. On every trip there are attacks, and we always have to be prepared to wage warfare from some unexpected enemy. It would be politic to not mention this aspect of mission work, but it is part of the reality of serving God. I thank God for my wife who has a strong faith of her own and who supports me when I am feeling overwhelmed. There have been many late nights in Belize when I have been venting my frustration to her about a certain individual and she has calmed me down and we have prayed for solutions to the dilemmas.

One of the most important assets in having a successful mission trip is having trustworthy Christian associates in the place where one is working. I have been blessed with several such people. Fr. Chris Glauncy was extremely cooperative and wise in his work with us. Over the years I have cherished his friendship and cooperation. We could never have accomplished the things we did without his support. It is vital to have a powerful ally in the region or country in which you are working as a visitor. The

Lessons Learned

principal of San Victor School, Maestro Benito Pantin, is a man that I admire greatly. He has been an invaluable ally and friend. I regret he retired after a lifetime of teaching and administering the school. My closest friend, who is my brother in Christ, is Armando Teck. He is a talented man with a generous heart who loves God and the people of San Victor. Armando and his wife, Amarilly, are two of the finest people I have known. They have worked tirelessly for the missions and their community. Before I went to Belize I did not know I had a Mayan brother, but then we found each other in San Victor. I wish I could convince Armando and Amarilly to move to the United States so we would be closer but they are committed to their community and would never leave.

My wife, Marcia, and I have taken other mission trips with other groups in different parts of the world. We would do much more of this but haven't the resources to do it. The beautiful truth we have discovered is that there are thousands of Americans serving Christ Jesus all over the world. Some take short trips; others live permanently at considerable sacrifice to themselves. They may be among the finest examples of faith in Christ, and their witness is changing the world in powerful ways. The saving power of their witness is transforming the lives of millions.

Some of my closest relations have never understood why I went on these missions, and why I was so eager to spend

Lessons Learned

money for the sake of the poor. However, the little that I did has been repaid in ways that I cannot adequately describe, except to say I have been richly blessed by God!

After more than two dozen mission trips to San Victor with over a thousand people, the many mission church groups have been inspired to form their own mission teams and operate all over Belize. I am very gratified by many churches that are committed to taking teams to Belize on a regular basis. I have heard wonderful stories about their incredible works of ministry. I have also had the privilege of joining some of these groups and enjoyed working with them without the responsibility of being in charge of the mission. My passion has been magnified and vastly expanded by hundreds of others also serving in the name of Christ. There are hundreds of other churches which have been working in Belize long before I began my mission work there, churches which will be working long after my time, bringing the love of Jesus to a broken world.

The gospels tell us Jesus took a small amount of bread and a few fish and fed thousands of people. That was a miracle. He asked his followers to do even greater things than he had done. I never imagined I would be a part of this kind of miracle. If you had told me that this would happen in my life, I would have thought you had lost your mind. But by the grace of God I have been a part of a

Lessons Learned

miracle that exceeds my wildest expectation. I was given this grace because I was willing and said *yes* to God. In a few years my name will be forgotten in Belize and by those who accompanied me on these mission trips. But that is not important. The fact is thousands of lives have been blessed by God because, along with many other people, we wanted to serve Christ Jesus and we did it. I know that is pleasing to God.

Lessons Learned

Lessons Learned

1. Jesus Christ is real and his love for all people must be made real and allowed to meet the needs of people. He did this in His earthly ministry and we are to follow his example.
2. Christian missionaries, including healing ministries, bring salvation, education, health, and healing to people who are underserved and sometimes do not have access to church, schools, hygiene, and modern medicine.
3. Blessing a family with a simple home gets them an important step forward in life to care for their family.
4. We have brothers and sisters in Christ around the world we never knew we had. What a joy it is to meet these Christian families.
5. Doing mission work is the greatest joy and blessing I have experienced in my Christian walk. What a privilege it is to serve Jesus Christ in this way.

Lessons Learned

Chapter 16 – God save the Church

Norwood, Ohio is a city within the city of Cincinnati, Ohio. In the past one hundred years it went from farm land to suburban to heavy industrial to rust-belt abandoned. Because of the large population of residents from Appalachia that traveled north seeking well-paying industrial jobs, the city had a reputation for being rough and racist. The German immigrants who had moved into the new suburban homes in the 1920's and 30's had mostly moved farther out into the newer suburbs. The city was dominated by acres of abandoned and soon-to-be demolished industrial sites. The main street was known for the numerous bars that had once catered to the factory workers. When I started working as a minister at Zion United Church of Christ in Norwood, twenty percent of the housing was government subsidized. Too many people in Cincinnati thought Norwood was a place to be avoided.

The faithful members of the congregation who mostly lived away from the immediate area of the church were loyal because of their family connections to the church. Two thirds of the congregation traveled some distance to attend church on Sunday. During the week the church

Lessons Learned

buildings were virtually empty except for a part time secretary and a housekeeper. One of my first impressions of the church was how lonely it was inside the building during the week. The only people I saw were the ones I went to visit in their homes. Most of the thousands of square feet of facilities were unused and neglected. It was evident to me that something had to change for this church to serve God's purposes and for the congregation to live the call to be Disciples of Christ Jesus.

The longer I served the church, the more I questioned whether churches should even own property. Is it necessary I wondered, to be invested in real estate to be a functioning church? At one time it had made sense. But I was the pastor of a huge facility with a small congregation and a rapidly diminishing budget. In the fifties and sixties this church had hundreds of worshippers on Sunday and built extensions of the buildings to accommodate the growing congregation and Sunday school. Now, years later, the church had become much like the industrial landscape around the church, fading into oblivion. Was my role to pastor the existing congregation and share with them the gradual death of the church like the previous pastors had done, or try something to reignite the flames of the Holy Spirit in the lives of the people? My plan was to prayerfully try new things and let God's Spirit of life and love prosper in this depressing place.

Lessons Learned

A man who was looking for a place to have Alcoholics Anonymous meetings came to me. I enthusiastically assured him they would be most welcome at this church. He told me there was a need for a place where the people could smoke because most the facilities that allowed them to use their space didn't allow smoking. I identified a basement storage room that could be used if we did some renovation. I took the proposal to the church council and they supported the idea. A group of us emptied the junk from the large room, cleaned it, painted it, wired new lighting, and furnished it. The room was perfect because it had a separate outside entrance so the groups could come and go as they pleased. In a couple of years we had five different groups meeting there.

A A is the most effective program for helping alcoholics achieve sobriety. I have attended many AA and Al Anon meetings (which are for friends and family members of alcoholics) and believe the Holy Spirit is very present and works through these groups and the twelve steps they promote for healing of this disease. Alcoholism is epidemic in the United States and affects even more millions of people – more than just those who abuse alcohol and other substances. The disease of alcoholism is a "thinking problem, not a drinking problem." God has used AA to help millions defeat the power of the disease and heal themselves of the delusions the disease

Lessons Learned

perpetuates. The first step to recovery is recognition by the alcoholic that they have no power over the disease and need the help of a higher power. When God is invoked in any way that a person calls on God, there will be a response. God is far greater than human language or human understanding. When a person's heart cries out to God, that call is genuine prayer and God responds compassionately. There may be just as much or more 'true church' in an AA or Al Anon group as there is in a traditional church. God loves the honesty of the broken addict and their desperate prayer for healing. I don't know how many hundreds of men and women found sobriety and healing in the basement of Zion Church. The increasing number of men and women attending meetings suggests the Holy Spirit was working there.

We started a prayer group that met on Thursday mornings. We met in the chancel of the church and sat in the choir lofts. We began by lighting the candles on the altar which was our way of acknowledging this was a sacred time and place. We shared prayer concerns for half an hour or more. The concerns ranged from joys to personal problems, family and congregation situations, and national and international difficulties. There were anywhere from four to twenty people in attendance. Sometimes we sat in silence for long periods of time. When everyone was finished discussing their prayer

Lessons Learned

concerns we all took turns praying. There were a few people who did not pray aloud by their own choice, but they were the exception. Sometime by noon we had all prayed and we concluded with the Lord's Prayer. Then we went to lunch. We had more fun at lunch because we had drawn so close sharing our prayer concerns. I loved this prayer group and rarely missed it. The people that attended that group became very special to me and to one another. We always prayed for our church and the church grew in faith and members. God answers prayer.

During the mid-seventies there was an energy crisis in which people were asked to conserve electric use by disconnecting non-essential lighting. The church had done that and never reconnected the lighting they had unplugged or disabled. The halls and rooms of the church were dark even when the light switches were turned on. So we went around reconnecting the lights and replacing burned-out light bulbs. It was wonderful how much brighter everything looked, except it showed the poor condition of the walls and floors. So we proceeded to paint every surface in the church and we stripped and waxed all of the flooring. The carpet in the social hall was terribly stained and we replaced it. The bathrooms were one of our first priorities and we decorated them with inexpensive prints. We installed soap dispensers over the

Lessons Learned

sinks and also installed paper towel dispensers. We hung curtains in the bathrooms.

Exploring the basement and attic of the church I found all kinds of framed paintings and prints. Most of them had to be cleaned of decades of accumulated dirt but they were beautiful when cleaned. We hung the newly discovered art and artifacts everywhere. Everyone seemed delighted with the discovery of their history except one man. He was a retired attorney and considered himself the leader of the church. After hanging some of the discovered art in the halls he came to see me at church. He announced that because I had not gotten permission from the proper committees for the hanging of pictures my services were no longer required and that I needed to pack my belonging and leave immediately. I had never been fired before so I was in shock. I had thought things had been going well but he announced "they" had decided to let me go immediately. He left my office and I sat their dumbfounded. After a while I decided to call a few of the people I had become attached to, to say goodbye.

When I spoke to them and told them what had happened they were angry with the man who had "fired" me. They told me to ignore him and they wanted me to stay and keep doing what I had been doing. After having the same conversation with a number of people I decided to take their advice. The Sunday service went ahead and never

Lessons Learned

was a word spoken about the incident. This happened in my first few weeks of ministry at Zion Church and I stayed there fourteen years. That man and I were polite to each other but never truly reconciled, unfortunately.

During my first year, I examined many different organizations in the hope of bringing them into our church facilities so that the buildings would be used during the week and we would be better stewards of the facility we inherited. I came across a ministry a few miles away that was looking for a new home. Fernside Center for Grieving Children was about a decade old and growing rapidly. We invited them to relocate in our facility and they eagerly agreed. Soon we had close to a thousand children and adult volunteers in our church weekly. Every weekday evening and Saturday the parking lot was full, and all the Sunday school classrooms were full of people healing from the loss of family members. All the services were free and the few paid staff members were funded by contributions. The church was alive and filled with ministries serving the community.

During my ministry at Zion there were typically a dozen to twenty people in nursing homes or were shut-ins. So a portion of every week was spent visiting these people as well as making hospital calls. My ministry to these people was empathetic listening and I prayed before each visit. Most of these people were very lonely and wanted

Lessons Learned

someone to take an interest in their lives. I became very attached to these wonderful elderly souls. To my continual surprise they often told me how much my visits meant to them, because I simply listened and prayed with them. I am certain the Holy Spirit made those visits significant for them. I believe that I represented to them something more than just a man. We had church together. Several times a year I would take Holy Communion to them and that was always a blessing for both of us. As often as possible I would try to get a church member to accompany me on visitations. This made the visits even more special.

One day a nursing home called and told me that a woman I had visited for many years was dying. One of my most faithful members named Ruth was in the office, and I asked her if she would go with me to be with the woman who was dying. We drove about fort-five minutes to the nursing home. The staff told us they had called the family but none of them were able to come. So Ruth and I sat with the dying woman for several hours. We prayed at times but mostly sat silently. There was Ruth and me quietly sitting in a room, listening to the intermittent breathing of a dying woman. When she died, it was very peaceful. We silently walked to the car and I started driving toward the church. I pulled into the parking lot of a large supermarket and told Ruth I couldn't drive and I

Lessons Learned

needed to walk around for a while. I was emotionally exhausted. She agreed and joined me. For half an hour we walked all over the supermarket. I spotted a display of giant sour pickles and asked Ruth if she liked sour pickles. She said she loved them. So I bought two pickles and we took them to the car. Sitting in the car we slurped and chewed on our sour pickles and began laughing. We couldn't stop laughing at the absurdity of eating these giant pickles. This turned out to be the antidote to our grief over the death of a friend and sister in Christ. We made it back to church safely.

The church has been described as a hospital for sinners and not a museum of saints. Some of the finest people I have known in the church made no pretense of being holier than thou. Don had retired from a lifetime of being a head of a cleaning crew at a major aircraft engine manufacturer in Cincinnati. He had not been very involved in the church during his working life, but now he was retired. He came to me and said he would give the church several days a week cleaning and fixing the building if he was given the support and freedom to do what he decided to do. I welcomed his contribution and for several years he spent at least three days and sometimes more cleaning, painting, and fixing things. Many times Don and I worked together late into the night on projects. We worked hard and enjoyed each other's company. We had

Lessons Learned

a few disagreements over how to do things but we always got over our differences. There was not a part of the property that was not worked on and improved by Don. After Don finished cleaning and painting he began promoting memorial stained-glass windows around the church. He had over a dozen new windows commissioned and dedicated. Then Don got interested in organizing special events. So he organized tea parties, cookie walks, pig roasts, and many other special events. Everything he worked on was successful because he was aggressive about getting many people involved. People would ask me what Don was planning next. More and more people were joining the church because it was a lively place and we were welcoming the community to be a part of our life. It is amazing how much can be accomplished by one person.

After over ten years of continuous activity in the church Don became ill. In a few months Don died of lung cancer. When I did the funeral service I had to stop when I was doing the eulogy for Don. I said I couldn't continue and I sat down. No one moved for a few minutes. I got up after I composed myself and finished the service. I had lost not only a dear friend but a man who really loved God and loved his church. Don told me often he did all this work for the church because he loved God and did it for God. I know he meant it. Don showed his love by giving of himself to the church because he believed in the church.

Lessons Learned

He was a humble man who would not speak in public and refused any public recognition. He told me several times that if I ever thanked him publically he would quit the church and I knew he meant it. I loved this man.

We started all kinds of small groups for people to grow in faith and discipleship. One of the groups I led every year was the Lenten study which met weekly during the Lenten season, beginning with Ash Wednesday and ending with Easter. We tried different themes each year and always had a simple meal to encourage people to come to the Lenten study during the week. The series I remember most fondly was inviting a different clergy to talk about their religious tradition each week during Lent. The speakers included a Catholic priest, a messianic Jewish rabbi, a Baptist preacher, an Assemblies of God pastor, a Swedenborgian minister, a Lutheran pastor, and an Episcopal priest. It was a terrific opportunity to learn and appreciate other Christian traditions. Everyone came away with a better understanding of our brothers and sisters in Christ Jesus.

There are so many good memories of people and events we had at the church that it would fill a whole book to contain them. The important point that needs to be emphasized is that the church, which is the Body of Christ, is a diverse group of people that all have their own relationship with God. The Holy Spirit has gifts for those

Lessons Learned

people to use for the building-up of the church. The purpose of the pastor is to equip the saints for ministry. My role was to help those individuals find their gifts and to use them for the building-up of the Body of Christ.

Not everyone in the church is called to be a part of a food pantry to feed the poor in the community, but there are some who have that calling. Harry had that calling and for many years, along with several others, worked every week at the food pantry that we supported with a few other churches in our community. They collected food, transported it, organized it, and distributed it to the needy. This was not glamorous work. The food pantry team, along with the other church supporters of the food pantry, was helping hundreds of families a month with groceries. At Thanksgiving, Christmas, and Easter, families were given all the ingredients for a holiday meal. Churches also organized gifts for the children. It was amazing what could be done through the cooperation of the faith community.

Our vacation Bible School averaged between one hundred to one hundred and fifty children a year. Some of the children were from our church, but many of them were children who did not go to church. It was a wonderful chance to teach them about the Bible and Jesus, many of them for the first time. We recruited Hispanic teachers from the surrounding neighborhood and had classes in

Lessons Learned

Spanish for the children of immigrants in the community. There was a growing population of Spanish speaking people in the vicinity of the church and I was trying to convince the church to hire a Spanish speaking pastor and start a Spanish worship service. Sadly there was little support for going in that direction, and that upset me. Try as I might, the resistance to opening the church to these neighbors was too strong. If we had gone in this direction God would have blessed this church, but they chose otherwise.

After fourteen years of serving this church it became evident to me the enthusiasm I had felt was gone and it was time for me to move to a new church or a new ministry. My passion for mission work had grown and it was clearly the direction God was calling me. I had also received a contract from Doubleday publishing to produce my book in the United States. It had been published in England in 2000 and had sold well. The expectation was that it would sell well in the US market. This would produce income to finance more mission work in Belize. So in 2005, I announced my plans to leave Zion Church and begin full time mission work in Belize. I started scheduling opportunities to preach in other churches in order to solicit support for the mission. We formed a board of directors and had an accountant working on forming a 501(c)3 non-profit corporation. I was planning

Lessons Learned

on having commitments from twenty or more churches on a regular basis to fund and send groups to Belize, which would become my ministry. Along with the book income I expected to have enough support to make this work and grow over time. I was certain this is what God wanted me to do and thought there was no reason why it would not prosper.

My first wife was completely opposed to what I was doing and was secretly making plans to end our marriage. In order to carry out her plans, she decided to keep me in the dark so she could make all the arrangements for her divorce from me. I went on a mission trip to the Amazon River with a group of medical people as the evangelist. It was the most amazing experience I ever had in ministry. Unknown to me, my attorney wife was emptying the house and the bank accounts in my absence. I soon went from the mountaintop to the depths of despair. God was still in control of my life, even though it was difficult to understand how. It was a time that demonstrated that our faith gives us the strength to endure disasters and find new directions for our lives.

Lessons Learned

Lessons Learned

1. The church needs to be a vital part of the community and not exist in isolation. Alcoholics Anonymous was one of the first groups welcomed into the church and all of them increased the work of the Holy Spirit.
2. The congregation needed to grown in Christian faith. We began prayer groups, visitation programs, Bible studies, and Lenten programs to deepen the discipleship of our members.
3. The church equips the Saints for ministry. We started small groups for fellowship and study. We adopted the Food Pantry for the City of Norwood. In cooperation with several other churches we served the poor directly.
4. Our vacation Bible School soon had over one hundred children. We expanded it to include Spanish speaking children and that brought new people into our church.
5. My passion for mission work was calling me to full-time mission work. My wife divorcing me changed my plans. God still had plans for me I did not know.

Lessons Learned

Chapter 17 – Jesus is Life

Jesus is the foundation of my life. "I am the way, and the truth, and the life" Jesus said. "No one comes to the Father except through me." This is unconditionally what I believe and what I live to the best of my ability. Some of my Christian brothers and sisters see this statement as an opportunity to exclude people from the hope of eternal life. I choose to see this statement as an invitation and as the hope of eternal life. These are not mutually exclusive approaches to the truth of Jesus; rather these are very different approaches to evangelism. This has made a dramatic difference in how I live my faith.

One day, for instance, Steve came to the church seeking money and I offered him some yard work around the church to earn a few dollars. He accepted the offer and was paid for his labor. He lived close to the church and I invited him and his family to visit us on Sunday to join us in worship. He said he would and left. I did not have high expectations that he would or would not accept the invitation. My skepticism was based on experience because of the location of the church in an economically depressed neighborhood where we frequently had visitors seeking money. When I first started pastoring, I gave small amounts of money freely from my pocket and discovered, over the months, that the more requests I

Lessons Learned

met, the more visitors I had. Everyone had elaborate stories to tell which always concluded with a request for money to buy something like food, gas, shoes, or to pay a bill. It seemed the word had gotten out that I was an easy mark. So after months of being an easy hit for these people I started insisting they earn the money by doing something to earn it. This dramatically reduced the traffic of beggars considerably. I also noticed that none of these people ever showed up at worship after my invitation for them to join us.

If people said they needed food I would get them food from our food pantry, and if they asked for gasoline for their car I would accompany then to the gas station and put some gas in their cars. If they needed help paying bills I sent them to an agency that our church supported along with other churches. There were special situations where it was appropriate to recommend psychologists who had sliding pay scales and other social services. There were a few occasions when I took people to the hospital and helped them get admitted. Rarely did I ever see any of these people again.

Steve would come around sporadically asking for work. I always found him something to do. Over time he introduced me to his wife and son. We had several opportunities to talk and he became increasingly honest with me. One day he admitted both he and his wife were

Lessons Learned

addicted to alcohol and drugs of all sorts. He was very proud of their son and wanted a better life for him. Steve did bring his son to our Vacation Bible School a couple of times. Steve and his family even came to worship on Sunday a couple of times. There were even a few occasions when Steve and I prayed together and asked God to help him change his life. How long Steve went without his drugs, I do not know. He was never interested in my impassioned pleas to take advantage of the AA programs at our church. Our relationship lasted many years with the same cycles in place. He would come seeking transformation and then returned to his additions.

One day I got a phone call from Steve, "I'm in the hospital," Steve told me. "They tell me I'm dying." Steve was in his late thirties, and apparently he was scared this was really the end of his life. I rushed to the hospital and met him in the intensive care unit. We talked and prayed together. He confessed his sins and asked Jesus to forgive him. I told him his sins were forgiven and that he was now right with God. The next day his wife called me to tell me that Steve had died. She asked if we could have the funeral service at the church, and I agreed. It was well attended by Steve's friends. I preached the Gospel of Jesus Christ to this congregation of people who were seemingly strangers to the church. My hope is that some

Lessons Learned

seeds were planted that day. God loves them and wants them to know Jesus and change their lives.

Part of my love for Steve had to deal with my own repulsion with what I saw Steve doing with his life, and what it also did to his wife and son. He knew he was destroying himself and he didn't want that for his wife or son, but the demons of addiction proved to be too strong for him. God wanted to give him strength and victory, but Steve always gave in to the other voices when the cravings got strong. The important thing to me was that he died in a state of grace, and I trust in that. My attempts to evangelize and convert him were not a waste, and I pray it had positive repercussions on his family and friends. If I had acted judgmentally toward him or his wife, which was definitely a temptation, I would never have had the relationship we established. Love should always speak the truth, but it must be done in a way that keeps the door open to hope. When we close the door of salvation on a person and they only are given condemnation, we have not served Jesus Christ. It is true that we hate the sin, but love the sinner. This is how I understand what Jesus did and asks us to do likewise.

My testimony about my near death experience and conversion have given me the opportunity to give numerous radio and television interviews. While I have never solicited these opportunities, I have almost always

Lessons Learned

responded enthusiastically to them. I have never been paid to do an interview and have only received travel expenses. There have been numerous occasions when I felt manipulated by the producers for their purposes rather than having an opportunity to testify to the saving power of Jesus Christ. The producers of The Phil Donohue show, for instance, invited me to tell my story. I was flown to New York and was seated in the green room (waiting room) to wait for my appearance before a live audience. There was one other man seated next to me. I learned that he was representing an atheist group from Chicago. After we were seated on stage, Phil asked me to tell my story. I tried to give a brief testimony, but the skeptic interrupted me and mocked me. It was difficult to not respond to him and to maintain my focus on my testimony. After the show was over the self-styled skeptic told me he believed every word I had spoken and that he only said the things he did because that was his role to contradict me. This may have been his attempt to apologize, but I wondered if it was sincere. He had tried to make me appear foolish and his attacks were personal and degrading. It felt like an ambush, and I had walked right into it. Some of these media productions made me feel like I'd been "rode hard and put up wet."

There were numerous occasions where a production company would come to Norwood Ohio and spend two or

Lessons Learned

three days interviewing me. On the one hand, I found this very flattering. On the other hand I was frequently disgusted with what would result after the editing process. During the hours of taping questions and answers, I would have mentioned Jesus Christ dozens or even hundreds of time, but when I saw the production on television there was never a single mention of Jesus' name. The heart of my testimony was left on the editing floor. Knowing full well that I had no control over the final product, I continued to do interviews with the hope that the message of salvation would get through whether the producer was sympathetic or not. My belief is that there is somebody watching or listening that is at a place in their life where they need to hear my testimony and they will call out to God. That makes it all worthwhile.

The Bible states in four different places that "anyone who calls on the name of the Lord shall be saved." If the Spirit of God can use my testimony to encourage someone to call out to God, then I have done my job. Only God saves people. No man or women saves anyone else. We can speak the message of salvation with the hope that it will be heard and acted upon by someone. The Holy Spirit needs a human witness. I know that God has used my testimony. This is the only reason I keep telling my story. I have told my story hundreds of time from large audiences

Lessons Learned

to individuals. I have never refused a request to tell my story even when I did not feel like telling it.

Many people are fearful they have sinned against God and cannot be forgiven because their sins are too horrible for God to forgive. By telling my story I demonstrate that such a notion is not true. When I share my witness, I have never confessed all of my sins. It would be a lengthy litany of sins and no one really needs to know all that garbage. My biggest sin was being an atheist and that is what I always confess. The sexual sins, the substance abuse, the blasphemies, and all the others are secondary to denying God. All sin is terrible, but denying God is the worst. I want people to know God forgives us when we repent and call upon Jesus to save us. It is a simple message and I hope that it gets through to people. It has been an unpleasant surprise that some Christians have failed to appreciate what I am doing. I have been attacked for being too liberal and attacked for being too conservative. It is beyond my understanding how some Christians have failed to understand the message to which I have been witnessing. My message is, Jesus saves!

Christian orthodoxy varies from group to group. I have studied theology and don't see anything I say or believe to be outside of the traditional orthodox Christian faith. I have asked other priests and pastors to tell me if I am outside of the historic tradition in any way and they have

Lessons Learned

told me I am within the historic tradition. The criticism has mainly come from lay persons who have decided they are theological police. It is futile trying to convince them otherwise, so I rarely make the effort. This may seem prideful, but I can't have a reasonable disagreement with a person who is seemingly incapable of a serious discussion of theology.

The beginning of any theological discussion is the recognition of our inadequacy in talking about God. We rely upon our Biblical understanding, our experience, and reason to venture into the mysteries of faith. Ultimately our faith is based on choices we make to assert our faith. We choose to trust or deny our experience, to take the bible seriously and study it or not, and to apply reason to our understanding or not; these are the choices we make. There is no scientific truth that proves our assertions. I have no interest in theological speculation for its own sake. My world is far too involved with real people seeking practical direction for their lives. When you are dealing with a mother who has just given birth to a stillborn child, I find myself trying to say a comforting word and not something stupid and harmful about God.

The following is another example of ministry in the real world. A young woman in my church committed suicide, to the shock of the congregation and everyone who knew her. To the rest of us, she had a happy life. She had two

Lessons Learned

beautiful children and a handsome husband. They had been members of the church as long as anyone could remember. Her deceased father had been a clergyman. She, herself, was an art teacher in the schools and did not appear to have any problems. However, this was what was on the surface. After the suicide, when I visited the family, I found out there had been a conspiracy of silence about what was really going on her life. She was under the supervision of a psychiatrist, was on medication, and had a serious drinking problem. From her husband and other family members, there was no question that she was drinking heavily and taking powerful antidepressant drugs. This can be a lethal combination. Everyone, including myself, felt terribly guilty because we did not know what she was doing to herself. My first reaction, after thinking about a funeral service for her, was, 'how do I deal with the terrible sin she has committed by taking her life?' This was the first suicide I had to deal with as a pastor. I decided I needed to learn more about suicide, so I began doing research. After several days of studying about suicide and praying for guidance, the Holy Spirit led me to understand that she was heavily influenced by the alcohol and anti-depressant drugs and had distorted thinking which led her to take her own life. Her decision was clearly wrong, and her distorted thinking was suffered under severe depression. The drugs and alcohol had been a lethal combination. The Spirit revealed to me

Lessons Learned

that this good Christian woman was not condemned by God for her terrible decision to end her life. Rather, she had sunk into a well of utter hopelessness and saw no way out. Because of her popularity and her deceased father's position, I knew it was going to be a well-attended funeral. Most importantly, she had two young children that needed to hear words of comfort and not words of condemnation. I preached the love of God and the mercy she received from a loving God because God understands such illness and despair. This message of a loving God reaching out to her was much appreciated by her family and friends. Everyone knew she had committed a horrible and stupid act by taking her own life, and the sermon helped explain why this may have happened.

I watched the children and the family while I preached and was sympathetic to their confusion and pain. They got some relief from the sermon and that was important to me. The father continued to bring the children to church and they grew up as well-adjusted people. It is very gratifying to have the inspiration of the Holy Spirit to present the love and mercy of God, as opposed to the meanness of the human instinct. This woman who ended her own life is God's own daughter, and God did not abandon her. The Spirit told me so.

One of the flourishing segments of our culture is the New Age movement. This is comprised of philosophies selected

Lessons Learned

from all the world's different religions, and cut and pasted together to suit the sensibilities of the particular devotee. One may find in New Ageism a bit of Hinduism mixed with a bit of Christianity, liberal splashes of Buddhism, and a dash of Animism. Every practitioner has their own opinions and theology, according to their own taste. It is completely individualistic and has complete disregard for authorities in the religious practices it borrows from. One might think of it as a mulligan stew of ideas. There have been several occasions when I have testified before New Age groups and have found them to be fairly hostile to traditional Christian doctrine. Try as I might to present the orthodox doctrine of Christianity, there is a strong emotional reaction against the tradition. I suppose many people attracted to New Age thinking are people who have been traumatized by some Christians sometime in their past and are seeking to distance themselves from the restrictive dogmas they were forced to accept.

New Age people are unconditionally open to any new insight into God as long as it does not agree with the traditional historic theology of Christianity. I have failed to make any impression on this movement or its adherents because my message is far too Christian for their liking. They much prefer a message with things that tickle their ears and delight their fancy. I am saddened by my failure to reach these people because they are seeking God and

Lessons Learned

are sincere in their desire. But they are wounded people who reject things that remind of a negative religious experiences from their pasts and accept, without discernment, the latest trends in popular new age literature.

One of the purposes of life is to learn discernment. To grossly simplify what that means is to learn what is of God and what is opposed to God. Sometimes the distinctions are obvious while at other times they are subtle. For example, child abuse is opposed to God, always. When and what kind of discipline is appropriate in child rearing is not so easy a question. To raise a child without discipline is opposed to God, but how much discipline is the perfect godly amount? This dilemma is why a strong relationship with Jesus is so vitally important. We don't know the answers to the questions we have every day. We need the guidance of the Holy Spirit, which is the Spirit of Christ, to show us the way, the truth, and the life. Without the indwelling love of God we are lost and not on our way to God.

My knowledge of Jesus comes primarily from the Gospels. These stories often challenge my thinking. How did Jesus, I ask myself, treat the people who were considered his enemies? In one story Jesus used a Samaritan man as a hero of compassion in comparison to some religious types of his culture. The Samaritans were despised by the

Lessons Learned

Jewish people. He embraced a Samaritan woman at a well to become the first evangelist. In another episode, Jesus healed a man for a Roman Centurion and commended him for his great faith. The Roman officer was hated by the Jewish people as a member of an occupying army. Jesus healed the daughter of a pagan idol worshipper from Syro-Phoenicia, someone he was lawfully supposed to shun. Jesus treated his "enemies" with love and respect in every instance. He even forgave the people who tormented and crucified him, which is mind bending. How are we as his followers to treat our perceived enemies? How do we respond to people for whom we feel hostility?

The only places in the gospels where Jesus seems angry with people are those where he is dealing with good and religious people of his own faith. He is so frustrated with the hypocrisy of his self righteous Jewish brothers and sisters that he rebukes and insults them. The follower of Jesus should not tolerate a sense of superiority over anyone. In full knowledge of our sinfulness and our inadequacy in relation to a Holy God, we see all persons on a level playing field. When we are given the grace of the conviction of our salvation, we have something we want to share with everyone and it is certainly not something to hoard or become prideful about. The most blessed moment in life is to help a sister or brother find

Lessons Learned

their own way into eternal salvation through a relationship with Jesus Christ as their Savior.

Jesus said, "Very truly I tell you, the one who believes in me will also do the works that I do, and in fact will do greater works than these." This is a life as it was meant to be.

Lessons Learned

Lessons Learned

1. Ministry is caring about one person at a time. There are times when the demands are overwhelming. We must not stereotype and prejudge people. Everyone is precious to Jesus.
2. Unexpectedly, a demand grew for my testimony about my conversion during my near death experience from atheist to Christian. This ministry has reached millions of people.
3. The more you do, the more you attract critics from every direction. I have tried to keep my eyes on Jesus and be faithful to Him alone.
4. Crisis creates an atmosphere of chaos. It is at these times we need to rely on God the most to find the peace and understanding the best serves to minister to our brothers and sisters.
5. Spiritual discernment is one of the most important qualities we need to cultivate in this lifetime. It is a daily struggle to identify God's will in our lives.

Chapter 18 – Homesickness Please

Homesickness is what I deal with every day to some degree or another. Starting on June 1, 1985 this world has been alien to me, and I have felt like I don't belong here. This is difficult to explain so I beg you to bear with me as I attempt to explain myself. When I was with Jesus, there was no deception and there were no secrets. Everything is known and out in the open. Jesus knows all our thoughts from the past to the present. The amazing grace is that He still loves us and is willing to forgive us our thoughts, words, and deeds. Not only does Jesus love us and tolerate our failings, but He actually enjoys our company. He likes us! In fact, He likes us and loves us more than we love ourselves. To be with Jesus is to be known fully and to know fully. He gives us the knowledge we desire. He is the source of everything and can access anything. To be with Jesus is to finally be oneself without anxiety or doubts. In His presence is to be complete, and that is why I say it is home. Home is where you are supposed to be known, loved for who you are, and completely at peace, safe and secure. To go where Jesus is, that is going home to where you really belong.

Lessons Learned

Heaven is far more wonderful than can be described. Everything good is in heaven, and there is nothing bad in heaven. Everything that was, and is, can be found in heaven to some degree. Heaven is vast and full of the wonders of God's creative mind. There is no limit to the delights of heaven. Of course the most magnificent part of heaven is the presence of God which is the center of everything. Why would anyone want to be on Earth when they could be in heaven? Why would we want to be in this world of struggle and suffering when we could be in the ecstasy of heaven? So when one speaks of being homesick, it is about going to where we belong and where we were created to live in eternity. This world is just a brief moment to determine whether we want to go to heaven or not.

You would think everyone wants to go to heaven. The reality is quite different. It is astounding how many people don't want to go to heaven.

There is an alternative to heaven and from what I experienced, it is hell. One of the big lies in our world is the denial of the existence of hell. Briefly, the following questions are assertions about the reality of hell. If heaven is a good and holy place why would evil people go to heaven? If God is just, why would God support evil behavior by rewarding people with no regard for the consequences of their actions? Jesus speaks about hell

Lessons Learned

more than he spoke about heaven, and we believe he spoke the truth, do we not? Doesn't the Bible state "we reap what we sow?" This makes sense to most people as wisdom. Since most people would acknowledge there is evil in the world, would they not expect that evil has its own place in the afterlife? If we know that it is necessary to incarcerate people for anti-social behavior, would God be indiscriminate about who goes to heaven? If an individual rejects God and what God represents in this world, is that person not rightly going to the place they desire absent from God? If God's love is not forced upon us in this world, why would God force love upon a person in the next world? In the cosmologies of the world religions there are hells with remarkable similarities, so this would make the concept of hell a universal truth, would it not? Our experience of life in this world informs us there are opposing forces that operate, and why is this not also true in our destiny after death?

There are many opinions about hell and there may be some truth to them because the variety of states of being may be infinite. There are also some statements about hell to clarify what we need to understand about it. First and most important is that God does not desire people to go to hell. God wants people to chose heaven and live accordingly. God gave us the gift of free will so that we may chose between God and evil, which is simply

Lessons Learned

opposition to God. What precisely happens to people in hell is unknown and there is much room for conjecture about the fate of people in hell. Hell exists in the realm of eternity so a moment in hell is an eternity and a billion times a billion years of earth time is still short of an eternity in hell. Do people degenerate in this state? That would be reasonable to assume but what would that mean precisely? That is unknown. Is annihilation the ultimate fate of people in hell? There is strong Biblical evidence to support that view. Are some people redeemed from hell after they have realized their sins? This is the understanding of the Orthodox Church. So the basic question is whether hell is a static state or a dynamic state of being. Since nothing in the world is static it would be logical to assume that hell is not static and there is change in the experiences of hell. No one knows for certain the answers to these questions.

Based on my experience that God gave me of hell I find the following characteristics of hell to be informative in how hell is understood. There appears to be no hope in hell, so it would be difficult or nearly impossible for a person to make a decision for escape from their situation. Hell is devoid of all the good things we enjoy in life – a complete absence of pleasure, joy, gratification, relief, or anything good. This would be experienced as overwhelming torment. People in hell have committed

Lessons Learned

themselves to the rejection of God in life and are equally or more committed to evil in hell, which makes them even more unlikely to change. All relationships in hell are predatory, so there is no one to influence a person in changing their minds. Hell is a state of being that mirrors the inner nature of a person. It is what they are in their hearts and where they belong. God gives people what they have rightly deserved, and God knows the truth. We use terms like judgment and punishment because that is the human justice system. God's justice is perfect and based on God's truth and omniscience. Therefore God's system is flawless and immediate. God's works are absolute and cannot be compared to the flawed human systems of justice and punishment.

Ultimately the question of eternal salvation and damnation is endlessly complicated but for the individual it is not so complicated. A person who has a saving relationship with God knows that, by their faith. As Christians we know the power of Jesus Christ to save us in spite of our imperfections. We have the promises of Jesus to rely upon. Without that relationship with God a person may have false hopes or no hope. They do not have the Christian assurance of salvation. It would be wonderful if everyone in the world knew what Jesus can give us so that we can live in confidence of our resurrection to heaven. Thankfully God knows what to do and how to do it so that

Lessons Learned

there is no mistake or injustice. God's decisions are always true and just.

Our lives are comprised of choices we make every day. Every moment of our lives are choices, both conscious and subconscious that dictate our next action. Choosing God is a conscious choice. Not thinking about God is a conscious choice and is a rejection of God every bit as much as consciously rejecting God. Since God is the source of being and everything that is grounded in that Source of Being, it is not optional to try to live in harmony with God to the best of our understanding. Thinking we can exist independent of our Creator is not only delusional it is rebellion against our Creator. This is the root cause and very nature of evil. People can deceive themselves into thinking they are good because they have separated themselves from God and the objective standard of true holiness. When we look at ourselves through the indwelling presence of the Holy Spirit we find ourselves in need of God's grace and we pray for that grace to lead us toward sanctification. Jesus promised us when we ask, seek, and knock for the good gifts, we will receive them. These are the gifts of the Holy Spirit and the fruits of the Spirit which God wants to give us. Love, hope and faith are the first three of the many gifts God wants to give us. These are the things we need to be asking of God.

Lessons Learned

Our purpose in this world is to glorify God by our thoughts, words, and deeds. We have been given the freedom to do whatever we wish, and the purpose of this life is to use our freedom to choose obedience to God which ultimately produces ultimate freedom. Freedom is to have choice and in the love of God there is unlimited choice. Opposition to God is ever decreasing choice. This can be understood by recalling what the reality of our existence is. We were made by God to fulfill God's purpose for our lives. As we strive to know and live our vocation, which is God's calling on our life, we grow in ability and opportunity to become instruments of God's will. We make decisions to refrain from behaviors that we perceive as not pleasing to God, and we cultivate behavior that we believe is pleasing to God. God gives us experiences that encourage us and help us to grow. We have small miracles and wonders happening in our life that become greater miracles and wonders. We know these supernatural events are not our doing; rather they are the work of God happening through us. We do not brag or advertise these great joys because they are not for us to exploit. God is glorified by our lives.

In my Christian walk I have seen and been a part of the same miracles that are in the Bible. No one needs to know what God has done by my willingness to be obedient to God. I thank and praise God for the experiences that I

Lessons Learned

have been blessed to be associated with. Most importantly, lives have been changed and people have chosen eternal life by my choice to be obedient to God's call. I know of nothing more important or rewarding in the world than to help a brother or sister find their Lord and Savior. May you be blessed as I have been blessed by bringing a lost soul to the good shepherd. This has been the cure for my homesickness. My thoughts on returning to heaven were about my own welfare and God has helped me overcome my selfishness to care more about others than about myself.

God has created each of us with strengths and weaknesses, which makes each of us unique individuals. To do God's will we have to honestly evaluate our abilities, and then develop these qualities for the purpose that we have been given by God. Life is about discerning what we are and what we can do effectively. God will both help us magnify the good qualities and diminish our faults, if we ask God for his help. The story of Christianity is God using insignificant people to do great things. The lives of the saints of the faith are individuals that initially were quite unimpressive, but by their obedience they became extra-ordinary saints. There are thousands of examples beginning with the disciples and continuing to today in persons like Mother Theresa. Many of the greatest people in the world are relatively unknown by

Lessons Learned

the world, but they are highly regarded by God. I have been enriched by love and friendship of many saints who have not known fame or fortune, but they are known by God.

One of the biggest obstacles to obedience to God is putting our pride, which is our will, ahead of listening to God's will. Humans are masters of self deception and I most definitely include myself in this category. There are no limits to how much we can rationalize anything to feed our cravings. This puts a huge barrier between us and God. Christians are just as frail as any other person and they fall into the same traps unless they are constantly vigilant against the wiles of the evil one. Sometimes it appears that the more a Christian progresses the more they are tested. There are times when it can be very discouraging because the challenges seem to be endless. Our faith is tested by these trials and tribulations. We become stronger in our faith by overcoming these trials. God is building us up for our destination, which is heaven.

"Why is heaven so unknown in this world?" was a question that I asked Jesus. He told me heaven is amazing and that if people knew the extent of that they would be rushing to get to heaven, disregarding what they are in the world to learn. So heaven is kept mysterious for us to concentrate on our life experience. We are not here to dream about "pie in the sky in the great by and by". Our

Lessons Learned

lives in this world determine whether we will go to heaven or not. How we live our lives is shaped by our faith or lack of faith in God. I want to go to heaven as much as anyone, but that is not why I have faith. I would do exactly the same as I am doing if there was no heaven. My faith in God is that I want to lead a life pleasing to God. That is my sole motivation. The promise of eternal life in heaven is the conclusion of pleasing God to the best of my ability. The purgation that I am going through and will endure to please my Creator is what life is about. That is the meaning of life, and with the help of God we will triumph. Everything we suffer through in this world is very small compared to the joy of knowing God.

Someday I will die. I don't know when or how. I hope I don't suffer too much at the end, but if that is necessary then I will do my best to pass that test. Knowing that the Son of God Jesus suffered helps me to know He is with me and I am with Him in suffering. When my spirit leaves my body I will be released from suffering and then I will be in the presence of Jesus. He said he will come to us and take us to heaven in John 14:3 and that is what I anticipate will happen when I die. Because I have experienced Jesus when I died in 1985, I look forward to the reunion. Others who have died before me will also be there to welcome me but first and foremost will be Jesus. My hope is that he will say, "Well done good and faithful servant.

Lessons Learned

Welcome into my Father's kingdom." He will be looking into my eyes with His loving and penetrating gaze, and I will know that He has me safe and brought me home. There will be much rejoicing as I reunite with family and friends. There will be people I have never met but only knew through their words.

My awareness of changes in my self-image will gradually begin as my sense of my mortal body fades away and I become aware that I am subtly transforming into my immortal body. The eternal body is made of energy that is completely different from the matter we have known in this world. We will become increasingly aware of a totally different universe where the physical laws we knew are no longer applicable. Fortunately we will have our family and friends to guide and instruct us during this transformation. We will have unceasing questions about heaven and what is happening to us that will be answered, often leading us to more questions. By the faith we have cultivated in our lives we will have no anxiety about our transformation. We know it is all good. The analogy that can best describe this process is the caterpillar turning into the butterfly – the traditional symbol of resurrection. During this process of metamorphisms we will dissolve our old self to become a dramatically different new self. This process is gradual and painless and is something to be anticipated as we become

Lessons Learned

more like Christ Jesus. We will become aware of the infinite possibilities of our new life and will want to do what God knows is best for our continuing development. In heaven there is no fatigue, so we will be energized to live more fully than we have ever imagined. We may want to do, contemplate, or learn something according to what we feel is necessary to more perfectly know God's will for us. There will be no anxiety about time because time does not exist as we understand it. We will have all the time of eternity.

In heaven we grow in love and wisdom. We have access to all knowledge and it becomes part of us. We bring our particular creativity to heaven to become part of the continuing creative process of the creation. Without God and God's people actively creating, there would be nothing. The creation is a process that involves God and those who have joined their will to God's will. Jesus compared this to a symphony orchestra where God is the composer and conductor and the saints are the individual voices and instruments, each adding their own nuance to the symphony. One has to be highly evolved to be a participant in the heavenly choir of creation. But one has all the time in eternity to achieve this honor. The saints are given position of responsibility over the worlds and supervise the development of souls in their discrete ways. Our world is managed, but the interference always

Lessons Learned

respects human free will. If the angels had their way they would constantly interfere with human conduct, and we would be simple tokens in a play. This is not allowed and chaos is given an opportunity to run its course to keep the human character free to develop. The important governing principle is that God is ultimately in control and God's purpose is good, whether we can understand it or not.

The faith and trust we develop in this world is the quality that God is seeking in us. God's love is made real in the way that we practice that love in our lives. Jesus says, "You will know them by their fruits" in Matthew 7:16-20. If you want to be secure in your salvation, then be certain that you are bearing good fruits. This is how we must evaluate our lives and make the necessary corrections. The question of fruitfulness is also extremely helpful in spiritual discernment. Look at the government, evaluate the church, examine your family and friends, and most especially, rigorously look at the kinds of fruits that are being born. If you find bad fruits are the products of what you're evaluating, walk away from it. If it is barren of good fruits, there needs to be serious change. If there are good fruits that are building the kingdom of God in this world, rejoice and carry on with the power of the Holy Spirit to guide you.

Lessons Learned

Lessons Learned

1. Our true home is heaven. When we learn anything about heaven we yearn to go there. Our purpose is to prepare ourselves and encourage others to be candidates for heaven.
2. The only alternative to heaven is hell. There are conflicting opinions about hell. Hell is separation from God and all the good God represents. Denial of hell is either foolishness or deception.
3. Salvation is faith in Jesus Christ as our Savior. We can live confident in his promises of eternal life.
4. While we are alive in this world we must learn God's will to the best of our abilities. This needs to be the primary focus of our lives.
5. When we are taken to heaven we will be transformed. We will become perfected and become more like Christ.

Chapter 19 – Image of God

We are made in the image and likeness of God. So it is written in Genesis 1:26. Books could be filled with speculation about the meaning of this statement, but I want to address this from a simply personal perspective. Since the Bible states that God is spirit it is clear that image and likeness means we are made in the spiritual likeness and image of God. Some of these qualities include consciousness, reason, imagination, discernment, creativity, and the capacity for love. These qualities make us different from the animals. We also have all the characteristics of animals such as sexual desire, instinct to dominate, and insatiable appetites. We have these additional qualities that we may cultivate or choose to ignore. Jesus showed us what being a human truly is. Jesus is the first perfect human, and that is what every person should aspire to be. With the power of the Holy Spirit we are capable of experiencing the life God intends for us. Lacking the Spirit of God we are destined to be little more than sophisticated animals fighting to satisfy our cravings.

From childhood we may have been fortunate to have godly qualities instilled in us by our parents or teachers. My mother wanted to be an artist more than anything else. Her father who immigrated to the United States and

Lessons Learned

grew up in poverty considered my mother's ambition to be impossible and forced her to become a nurse. In that time and culture, she had no choice but to obey. She practiced nursing all of her life and did a good job in that noble profession. She never lost her love for art and occasionally stole a few hours to paint during the week around her full-time work of nursing and raising a family. Some of my earliest memories as a small child are watching my mother paint. It was magical watching my mother create something beautiful out of nothing. She was eager to share her materials and joy with me and I was drawing and painting before I went to kindergarten. This has been a great joy to me all of my life.

When I went to school I was identified as the little artist because I loved it and I was good at it. My teachers called me talented, but I knew the secret of being talented. Talent was the result of doing something far more than anyone else. The skills to draw and paint are acquired from thousands of hours of practice. Probably anyone can achieve these abilities if they are willing to do the work. For me it has always been a labor of joy. For other people it is not so rewarding and they're not willing to invest the time and energy into developing the skills. There may be some genes that are more favorable to certain abilities than others but they are far less important than desire. During my twenty years teaching art at the university I

Lessons Learned

consistently witnessed the development of the ability to draw and paint by people who had very little "talent." The failure of people who showed talent in the beginning was directly a result of their lack of effort to develop.

As a teenager in the late nineteen fifties and sixties the art world was in turmoil. Abstract expressionism was all the rage and was heralded as the ultimate evolution of art. In that era the trend in art was away from representation to abstraction. As an immature artist this was exciting and disturbing. In my painting I tried everything from portraits to just throwing paint onto canvas. When I went to San Francisco I was intrigued by the Bay Area figurative movement which was represented by the work of Richard Diebenkorn, Elmer Bischoff, and David Parks. When I arrived in 1966 I discovered they had all moved away, but I did study with some of their students. The biggest influence on my painting was Joan Brown who had studied with Diebenkorn, Bischoff, and Parks. However, she had moved from Abstract Expressionism to a representational style that was entirely her own. She stressed "painting from the heart" and being indifferent to trends in the art world. I followed her example and painted without belonging to any school other than the school of eccentrics. When I went to graduate school at the University of California Berkeley I finally had the opportunity to study with Elmer Bischoff who encouraged

Lessons Learned

my eclectic direction, an opposite to my peers. He gave me the confidence to pursue my own style of representation painting.

These were the late nineteen sixties and early seventies and the art world was embracing and discarding art movements yearly. It was becoming clearer and clearer that art was a commodity in the world of fashion, and work was made famous for a brief period of time and then forgotten so that the latest trend could be exploited for the gain of investors. Artists were pawns in a business of buying and selling that had nothing to do with values or meaning. Those of us who were putting our hearts and souls into our work had no place in the art world and found ourselves completely alienated from it. As mentioned earlier, our work was laughed at by the gallery owners and there was no opportunity to show or sell our work. It became obvious that the only way to make a living connected with art was to become a professor of art, and that is what I pursued.

My personal work reflected the state of my soul. My work explored the themes of eroticism, violence, the absurdity of life, and narcissism. These themes were who I was at that time and the exploration of them revealed the truth of my existence. I have since destroyed many of these paintings because they disgust me. Not all of the works of

Lessons Learned

that time were horrible, but generally I am ashamed of my efforts.

In 1970 I received a one year position as "artist in residence" in Roswell, New Mexico. This was the happiest year of my life. Immediately upon arriving in Roswell I was fascinated with the light and vastness of the desert. It was like living by the ocean with a horizon that stretched forever. Most of my paintings were landscapes of the surroundings on the northwest corner of Roswell. I found it beautiful and tried to capture it just as it presented itself to me. The quality of light and space were my focus. The paintings were typically large and very simple.

I then returned to Berkley to complete my Masters of Fine Arts degree. After the tranquility of New Mexico and the congestion of the Bay area, the climate of politics was such a contrast to the serenity of New Mexico that it was disturbing. The ability to be totally focused on a painting for days at a time was not possible in Berkeley. What I had found as an artist in the desert was almost impossible to regain back in school. My paintings had become an emersion into a zone of creation that transcended time and space for me. This was pure contemplation of being through the visual senses. Although I was not thinking of God at that time my pursuit was indirectly trying to appreciate God.

Lessons Learned

God is revealed in the creation. This was what I was seeking in my immersion into the world of light and space. The subject matter was simply being in the present without any other agenda. Later in life I came to realize that this is precisely what prayer is and should be. This zone of creativity is completely present without distraction or expectation. So I look back and think of myself as being in contemplative prayer without fully knowing it. In this state there is no self consciousness. There is no sense of time and there are no distractions. In this state we move beyond our normal state of consciousness and enter into a higher consciousness.

One other type of activity that this can be compared to is an athletic experience. When I was in high school I threw the shot put, discus and javelin. To do these events one has to practice and practice so that when you throw in competition, you are so prepared that the only preparation is absolute concentration on effort and not on technique. I use to have to empty my mind of everything to be totally focused on putting all of my energy into the throw, or what we called the explosion. The explosion began in the feet and burst up the legs into the torso and out the arms. The goal was to put every ounce of your being into this well rehearsed motion with the perfect angle and intensity. When it was good you knew it, even before the object left your hand. I

Lessons Learned

remember on my best throws I didn't look after them because I knew already they were good. This all happened in a few seconds of intensity, but it is similar to the zone of painting when it is at its best.

This is not to be mistaken for loss of consciousness; rather, it is just the opposite. It is higher consciousness. In the zone means one is seeing and feeling the smallest detail in relationship to the whole. One makes thousands of decisions without hesitation because the interaction between the creator and the creation are mutually responsive. I called it the place where the painting painted itself. This state of creativity is participation in the consciousness of God. In this world there is rarely a state that is closer to being one with God. There are situations that emotionally feel close to God, but they are generally fleeting. The zone of being one with God is typically more lasting and transcends feelings. The contemplative state is ineffable. It cannot be described as feeling, except to say there is serenity about this state that is unlike any other. One does not have to do anything to be in a contemplative state of unity with God. I have achieved this state of mind by doing no activity. It has occurred when listening to certain music, such as Bach. I find looking over a body of water to be conducive to achieving this state. When you experience this state of mind you yearn to live in that place always, but unfortunately the

Lessons Learned

world doesn't allow that serenity to always be possible. So I strive to return as much as possible to where I find God's presence.

It's not possible to accurately depict God, because God is far beyond representation. So the next best approach is to create situations where we can find God. Music, art, nature, and architecture are portals to help take us to that place where we can contemplate God. Churches and chapels are just those kinds of places, or should be. There is something spiritually unique about being in a sacred place and seeking God. One of the many reasons why I love the church is because I have experienced God in church on many occasions. This is something that many people have experienced, and it is disturbing that everyone who attends church doesn't have this experience. Is the reason why some people do not experience the holy in church because they are not giving themselves over to the possibility? Letting go of control and expectations is essential to experiencing the sacred in church. Finding God's presence is impossible when we demand it, and possible when we are at peace and open to God being present to us. God is most present when we give ourselves over to the sacred rather than trying to force something to happen. The Bible says be still and know that I am God. This is the only approach that works.

Lessons Learned

Sometimes we say we got lost in a piece of music or art. Of course this expression really means just the opposite. Yes we lost our ego consciousness, but we found ourselves in relationship to something greater. To lose our ego-centric self to a higher consciousness is finding ourselves in relationship to God. The aesthetic appreciation of the sublime is finding God, and worship can be this opportunity. Worship is giving one's self over to something greater. Letting go of self consciousness to dwell in a higher consciousness is true worship and this is where we are truly present to God.

Watching the sun set over the ocean, listening to Mozart, painting, and worshipping in church, are all entryways to the same place. This is where we connect with God. God wants to connect with us, but do we make the effort to make that connection? God is Holy and beyond the ordinary things of this world so we must seek God in a state of consciousness that is beyond the ordinary realm we inhabit. In other words we have to go to where God is, and not to demand God perform for us in our mundane world of fears and desires. The Bible says the fear of God is the beginning of wisdom. The fear of God is reverence or having an appreciation for God. That is awe. This does not mean we are to be afraid of God; rather we are to approach God in humility having an understanding that God is our Creator and we are mere creatures.

Lessons Learned

When Jesus was asked by his disciples how to pray, he gave us The Lord's Prayer. It begins with a profound statement of who God is. This acknowledgement of God is how we must begin our approach to art, to worship, and to life. Without this knowing of who God is and who we are in relationship to our Maker we will get nowhere. The purpose of religion is to help us transform ourselves into a person who lives in closer relation to our Creator and to one another.

The holidays/holy days of the Christian church are opportunities to grow in both a rational understanding of the faith and to experience an esthetic appreciation through worship of God. One of my favorite rituals is the sharing of the light of Christ at Christmas Eve services. We slowly dimmed the church lights at the end of the Christmas Eve service and sang "Silent Night". From the Christ candle in the middle of the Advent wreath we took a flame and passed it to members of the congregation. They in turn passed the flame to the person next to them until everyone held a lit candle in church. Looking out over the multitude of little candle lights, filling the church with beautiful light as we sang the simple hymn, filled me with the presence of God. This simple act involved all the senses and the action of the whole congregation in invoking God's presence. As an artist I considered this participation in worship to be a great work of art. When

Lessons Learned

we said, "Jesus Christ is the light of the world, and anyone who believes in Him shall not walk in darkness, but have the light of life", we experienced it fully. Our faith was made real and our faith was confirmed in this ritual.

This is where art and life meet in the simple rituals of the church. Holy Communion is another example of an act that can be a sacred moment with God. That is why we call it a sacrament. Part of being an ordained minister is the responsibility of the proper presentation of the sacrament of Holy Communion. There are prayers and procedures that must be observed for the sacrament to be observed and understood. In communion we remember what Jesus did, we participate in what Jesus is doing, and we look forward to what God is going to do. The sacrament transcends time and space. The elements are symbols of both the basic elements of life and the spiritual elements that are life in Christ Jesus. In our reverence for these simple elements we are invited to experience the Holy. To put it simply we are asking God to inhabit our lives with this gesture of taking the bread and wine. We acknowledge that what we are asking for is the Body and Blood of Jesus Christ. If we come to this sacrament in faith it is precisely what we ask for in faith. It is not our power at work in the transforming work of Holy Communion; rather it is the power of God working in us through the Holy Spirit. It is an opportunity to experience

Lessons Learned

the sublime presence of God in the community of God's people. This sacrament is art at its highest expression.

The more I learned about the Christian faith, the more I came to understand and appreciate the beauty of its traditions and expressions. Artistic activity is far more than making art as a commodity. It is self evident that the art can be the pursuit of God to some degree. Art is a creative approach to any human activity and anyone can be an artist in what they do. A pie can be a work of art and so can a well dug foundation. If we thought about attempting everything we do as an opportunity to do it as beautifully and as creatively as we can, our lives will be enriched as artists. When we make our work a conscious choice to connect with God so that all that we do becomes our humble way to glorify God, we will find ourselves living in the presence of God.

Too often we find ourselves alienated from God, and that begs the question of who has moved. Has God abandoned us or is it we that have moved away from God? The truth is, God does not move away! God is always present and it is up to us to seek God. When we respond to a child in a loving and creative way we connect with God in love. When we make our routine tasks of life our little works of art, we find God in the ordinary. When we take the time to contemplate the beauty of the world around us, we see God is everywhere in everything.

Lessons Learned

This is how we find the reality of God in the person of Jesus. The gospels present us God in human form and with a man who completely embodied the living God. We lose ourselves in becoming a new person through the Spirit of Christ that we invite into our hearts and minds. It is the Spirit of God, now living in us, that gives us life.

Lessons Learned

Lessons Learned

1. As we cultivate our talents we draw nearer to God. God made us to become more like God.
2. The world can pervert and distract us from our union with God. We cannot serve God and the world.
3. When we connect with God through the use of the talents we have been given, we enter into a state of higher consciousness. We can increase in this state of sublime awareness through the pursuit of our talents.
4. Worship presents many opportunities for entering into the presence of God. The Holy presence is magnified in the traditions and rituals of Christian worship.
5. The Holy presence is within our reach in simple routines of life. If we seek God in our everyday lives, we will find God.

Chapter 20 – Call Upon the Name of the Lord

"Everyone who calls upon the name of the Lord shall be saved", is repeated three times in the Bible – in Romans 10:13, Acts 2:21, and Joel 2:32. If this profoundly clear verse is repeated three times in the Bible by three different authors it must be important. I called out to Jesus when I was in hell and Jesus came and took me out of that place and gave me a new opportunity at life. I would urge anyone who has any doubts about their salvation to call upon the name of the Lord immediately. There is urgency to doing this because you do not know when it may be too late, and the benefits to having a personal relationship with Jesus Christ are so great you will want to enjoy those gifts of the Holy Spirit as soon as possible. This is the day of salvation. In this chapter I am suggesting in detail precisely what one must do for this to be effective. An insincere or less than heartfelt plea is not going to produce any results. God is not to be deceived.

When I was dying in the most horrible place imaginable, I cried out to God. I was a piece of filthy corruption and God, in the person of Jesus, came to me. He touched me and made me whole. Jesus filled me with a love I never knew was possible. He transported me out of that place and helped me understand my life. He gave me the

Lessons Learned

possibility of a completely new life. Jesus will do the same for you.

If you know you are a sinful person, and can admit to that fact, that's terrific because that is the first step in calling upon God. God not only appreciates honesty, God demands honesty. The truth is, God despises hypocrisy and lies. If you are unaware of your sinfulness you are either delusional or have deceived yourself. I have never met anyone who claimed to be perfect and it is improbable that such a person exists. It has been said, "The unexamined life is not worth living." By a thorough self-examination everyone will find more sins than we care to admit. If we compare ourselves to a Holy God and the perfection of Jesus, we fall far short of any semblance of goodness. Sin is the intentional separation from God. We sin in thoughts, words, and deeds. All people sin frequently and have separated themselves from God. If you are unwilling to accept this, you are in desperate need of pastoral consulting. Fortunately, this type of narcissism is not common and if you have gotten this far there is hope for you. To approach God with an open heart, one has to demolish all the disguises and deceptions we employ to maintain an ego that is alienating us from the truth. That ego is a major barrier to receiving God. Take an inventory of all the wrong things you have done, and all the ways you have failed to do the

Lessons Learned

things you should have done. Yes, there are reasons why you behaved the way that you did, but these do not excuse the choices that you made. The beginning of receiving God into your life is an honest assessment of your life. This confession is between you and God. If you need an intercessor than by all means seek one. This first step of making a searching critical confession of sin is essential to a relationship with God, and without it there will not be a relationship.

There are several reasons why this is so difficult and the following are a few explanations. We always want to avoid anything that causes pain, and the worst pain is emotional pain which is usually more difficult to handle than physical pain. Pain in the body can be identified and objectified. It is even possible to have serenity while experiencing extreme physical pain. By contrast, emotional pain can become our identity; in other words, when we suffer from emotional pain we believe we are that emotion. When we are depressed we think we are worthless. When we are elated we think we are happy and worthwhile. We are not our emotions, but the emotions can be so overwhelming that we delude ourselves into thinking that is who we are. The remorse we feel at confessing our sins is painful and will make us feel miserable. This may lead us into hopeless thoughts. Why would God care about a wretched person like me?

Lessons Learned

God will reject me if God knew what I was really like. I am unlovable and deserve my damnation. These examples are typical thoughts we have when we face our sins. They are all false, and may be lies that have been planted into our minds by destructive relationships in our past. These voices are the enemy to our wholeness with God and need to be seen for what they are. They are hurtful lies said by dangerous influences to demean and often to control us. God knows us better than we know ourselves so there are no secrets we can keep from God. God wants us to receive His love. We are the ones keeping the barriers up, preventing us from knowing that love. God wants us to be in heaven no matter what we have done. God has suffered and died for us so that we may know God's forgiveness in the person of Jesus.

We hold on to our old ways because that is who we think we are, and it is fear of the unknown which prevents us from letting go of the old self so that we might embrace a new self. We are often asked, "How is that working for you so far?" So we defensively reply it is working well enough, even when we know it's not working well at all. It is easier to take the path of least resistance than risk change. We have everything invested in our hard-won ego; why take the chance of tearing down the walls and letting a higher power take control? This is why it ofte

Lessons Learned

takes a crisis to realize we are at the crossroads of life, and it is time to make a decision which way to turn.

Thankfully God gave me an opportunity to experience the lowest pit of existence in my time in hell because that shattered my ego and gave me the opportunity to reflect on my life. That led me to call upon Jesus who gave me a new life. Hopefully you will not have to descend to those depths before you turn to God. It is helpful to realize that we are not determined by our thoughts, and we can change. In fact with the assistance of the Holy Spirit we are capable of total transformation. God is patient and understanding of this struggle and will help us change gradually, but only with our cooperation in the process. God is not going to force us to do anything; rather God is going to challenge us to be brave and trust in the process of transformation, which is called sanctification. After my conversion I was shocked and dismayed at my failures to be a perfect saint. I have battled many old demons and with the help of God have been victorious much of the time. The demons of rage, lust, egotism, greed, control, d many others have tried to defeat my life in Christ, and have fought many times. By the power of the Spirit of which lives in me, they cannot win. These demons persistent and devious but the power that lives in stronger and we are victorious. The process of tion is a lifelong struggle, but worth every ounce

Lessons Learned

of energy it takes to keep on fighting the good fight. It is not magic, striving to live by the Spirit of God. It is the very essence of being human as a child of God.

We hold on to our old self, no matter how flawed we know that we are, because we believe we will be losing everything we have invested our lives in attaining. The truth is, when we receive Jesus as our Savior, we will begin to question what we have control over. Everything we have has been won at a cost of lives and now we question if these things are what we should hold on to. All of my life I passionately wanted to be an artist and I was having success as an artist and an art professor at the university. When I felt called to the ministry in the church it was a long and difficult decision to let go of my career as an artist and professor to study for the ministry. I miss being around college students and I do miss the income at times when I am trying to make ends meet. There are no regrets leaving the university and serving the church because I have grown much more in the ministry than I would have, staying in the security of being an artist and teacher. The joys and tears of ministry have forced me to become a person I could not have imagined years before. My wife of forty years left me because she despised the new person I became and wanted to have nothing to do with me. This was extremely painful for me and I felt devastated and abandoned by God. With the help of A

Lessons Learned

Anon and the church I recovered and was blessed with a Christian woman who loved me as a pastor. We have a marriage I never imagined possible. What a joy to be evenly yoked with a follower of Christ. We suffer when we lose the old things that we think we cannot live without. God has better things for us when we let go of the old and follow the Holy Spirit to the new. What appears to be loss becomes gain. It is often said, "for every door that closes new doors are opened."

Everyone needs support, and God is not only mindful of our need for support but has provided multiple means for us to have all the support we need. When we are ready to ask God in the person of Jesus to be our Savior we are not alone. If we chose to ask Jesus to come into our life, we need support to take the next steps. If we ask Jesus to be our Lord in church we need to become an active part of that church for support. Everyone needs the body of Christ, which is the church. The right church is where you are nurtured and grow in faith. Brand new Christians are vulnerable as new-born babies and they need the love and strength of mature Christians that are found in the church. Mature Christians are active in the church because they both need the church and serve in the church to help others. They are there to give as much as they are there to receive. New Christians are all about what they want to get from the Church, not yet strong

Lessons Learned

enough in their faith to give. The church has a designated pastor but there are many pastors in the church who are not designated with the title. When you have asked Jesus to come into your life you need to become part of the Body of Christ. I do not believe that Christians exist in isolation from the Body of Christ. The church is a dedicated body of people doing the work of Jesus Christ. Sadly, churches are imperfect institutions because they are made of people. People bring all of their human frailties into the church and those flaws can be a discouragement to the new believer. If you are looking for the perfect church you need to leave this planet because they don't exist here. If you are unhappy with certain things in the church, either help to change them and make the church better or go to a church that is more suitable to your needs. It is easier to improve the church than it is to change other institutions. Try changing the government, schools, hospitals, legal system, businesses, or any other institution. The church is an institution that can change, and with the dedication of any individual, it will change much of the time. The prayer to receive Jesus Christ is linked to venturing into the life of the church, which is the Body of Christ. One cannot receive the Spirit of Christ and reject the church which is what God established to be the Body of Christ in the world.

Lessons Learned

There are widely diverse styles of worship in the world and they are all good for those who respond to that type of worship. Find the worship that works for you. One style of worship is not better than another; they are just different for different tastes. It is important to be involved in Bible study through the church. There are unlimited types of Bible studies and we are each responsible for finding the kind of study that suits our needs. If you don't find one to your liking then start one the way you want it to be done. Ask God to identify a ministry or mission of the church that you can serve in, to use your gifts for the building of the church. Some people have a passion for charitable works, some have a passion for hospitality, some have musical gifts, some are gifted for teaching, some have administrative gifts, and some have a passion for maintenance. There are many gifts the church needs and you have a corresponding gift to give for the church to be the Body of Christ. This involvement in the life of the church is not optional because it is God's program of sanctification. How many people have left the church because somebody said something they didn't like or did something they disapproved of at the time? Would you quit your job because you were disappointed in some unpleasant incident? It is astounding how little people tend to be forgiving in church, where the premise of forgiveness has created the church. We are to be forgiving as God has forgiven us.

Lessons Learned

God has given us a collection of literature that has been identified as sacred over centuries. This literature called the Holy Bible contains material that has been known to be inspired by human's interaction with God. This means the Holy Spirit has revealed truth in this literature. Some of the literature is easily understood and some of it is mysterious. Without the assistance of the Holy Spirit it is not appreciated for what it truly is – the word of God. Without prayerfully asking the Spirit to reveal the word of God in the Bible, it is not of much value because the living word is not revealed. The Bible can speak God's word to us if we approach the Bible prayerfully. The more you seek God in the Bible the more you will find God speaking directly to you. It is unique literature and there is nothing else in the world like it. The more you prayerfully invest in the word the closer you will be drawn to God. Most importantly, through the Bible you will know Jesus as the perfect revelation of God who lived, died, and was raised from the dead. If you want to have an intimate relation with God you must know God as God has chosen to Reveal God's self to us. The Bible is the source for knowing God and the ultimate source of the mystery unveiled in the Gospels, which tell us about Jesus. Prior to the life of Jesus, God revealed much about God in nature and what God wanted us to know about our relationship with Him. In the Gospels we get the complete understanding. In the letters of the apostles that follow

Lessons Learned

we receive understanding from those who knew Jesus. The Bible contains the wisdom and the truth that is necessary to be a child of God. The more you study, the more the Spirit of God in you will help you understand.

A follower of Jesus Christ must be a student of the Bible. The Bible is the authority for our faith and for the church. The Bible has been used in perverse ways by people for their own purposes. That is not a reflection on the value of the Bible; rather it shows the perverse nature of people to take something meant for good and uses it for evil. The ultimate theme of the Bible is portraying God as a loving God who cares deeply for humans. This story is complicated and takes study to comprehend its meaning. There are thousands of books written about the Bible which help us understand its true meaning and the context in which it was written. It is necessary to have some understanding of the history and culture of the scriptures and what the purposes of the different books in the Bible intended to convey. Students of the Bible can begin to deepen their knowledge by reading commentaries by scholars to broaden their comprehension. When I went to Seminary we studied the scriptures in the kind of detail that fascinated me. I would have been perfectly happy to have spent the rest of my life studying scripture, but I was called to pastor and not

Lessons Learned

to begin a new academic career. Let God reveal to you the heart and nature of God that is in the Bible.

When one asks Jesus to come into their life it may be dramatic or it might not. Sometimes people expect spiritual fireworks and question the efficacy of the event if it doesn't meet their expectations. This is not how it works. The reason that I wrote about becoming part of the church immediately after the section on confession is to emphasize the importance of growing in the faith. The brand-new Christian needs lots of support and guidance. There are many wiles of the evil one and they will be used to distract and undermine a new Christian. The novice needs the Body of Christ for protection and direction. Falling in love with Jesus is not an infatuation which blows hot and cold. The love of Jesus is intense and grows in time to become the most important thing in our lives, and this happens along with increasing knowledge and wisdom. Our accepting of Jesus as our Lord is not a flirtation that depends on our feelings of the moment. Knowing and loving Jesus is a lifelong marriage that grows in ways we cannot anticipate. The best advice one can give to a new Christian is not to anticipate anything and let the Spirit of Christ surprise and delight you regularly. Let the church be your school and place of worshipping God. Keep mature Christians as your friends and let the Bible be your guide.

Lessons Learned

I ministered in churches for twenty-two years serving two different churches in Ohio. I love the church more now, than ever. There were times when an individual in the church upset me and it was difficult to know how to respond. I made many mistakes in my dealings with people and wish I had done it better. I do believe I did the best I was capable of doing at the time. I tried to do no harm and hope that I did some good. I was blessed by the people in the congregations that I served.

Building friendships with other clergy was and is a very important part of my life. I have gotten to know some remarkable men and women who serve churches. These people could have had successful careers in the world and made many times the money they made serving churches. Most of the clergy I know don't earn what public school teachers earn, and they retire with much smaller pensions. Clergy are on call twenty-four hours a day, seven days a week without exception. Since very few people have any notion of what clergy do with their time, the long hours clergy spend are not generally acknowledged. It is not unusual for a clergy person to spend fifty or more hours a week doing their work. Some clergy are more effective than others, and some are more gifted than others. There is no incentive to be in the ministry other than a faith in God. Clergy are receiving ever decreasing respect in our society. Clergy are painfully

Lessons Learned

aware of the diminishing regard in which they are held by our culture. It is hard to explain why anyone would want the job of being a minister. The fact is, really good capable men and women become ministers and persevere against the difficulties. It is an honor to serve with these people and I consider many of them my friends. Many churches would be better served if they supported their clergy rather than looking for their faults. Every clergy person has strengths and weaknesses, so it is more productive to build on their strengths and find ways to compensate for the weaknesses than to focus on the defects and ignore the virtues. The church is a team and not a corporation. It is most unfortunate that all churches do not appreciate their ministers more, so that they can realize their full potential in their call to serve Christ and His church.

As Christians we live in constant tension between the demands of the world and the will of God. This world is dominated by a spirit that is opposed to the will of God. To speak plainly, our culture is very bestial. Much of our society behaves like partially trained animals trying to gratify their base desires. We are all cognizant of our animal needs and desires, and I certainly include myself in this description of human nature, but there is more to being human. When we study the life of Jesus Christ in the culture of His time, dominated by the Roman Empire, it is not very different from our experience of being a

Lessons Learned

Christian in today's world. Yes, there are some important distinctions between today and two thousand years ago but there are also many interesting comparisons. One has to make frequent compromises to adjust to our world. For example, we live in a world that is in constant warfare, which is contrary to the will of God. We are all part of an economic system that distributes wealth so unequally there are millions starving to death while others have more wealth than some nations. There is enough food in the world for everyone. Millions of people starve. This is contrary to the revealed will of God in the Bible. We spend millions on cosmetic surgery while some die from lack of basic medical care. When we talk about the injustice in the world we are dismissed as crackpots. I have tried to speak about the poverty of the people I have lived and worked with in foreign missions, and I have sometimes met overt hostility from my church audiences. Sometimes it seems no one wants to hear about injustices in the world. Christians have made a huge impact on the world and we have much work ahead of us to make this world the way God wants it to be. With the help of God we can change the world.

My life was radically changed when I called upon the name of the Lord, and yours will be also. I am eternally thankful that I was given the opportunity to experience the consequences of my sinful life, and had the chance to

Lessons Learned

call upon Jesus. There is nothing we have done that God is ignorant of our doing. God knows our thoughts as well as our deeds. When we repent, God is eager to give us a new life to be the person we were created to be. God's plan of salvation is more than words. "For God so loved the world that He gave His only Son, so that everyone who believes in Him may not perish but may have eternal life." John 3:16 is a statement of faith and fact which summarizes the plan of salvation for each of us. The alienation people feel between themselves and God is not God's will. This separation is the result of the collective sin of humans. What more do you need to let go of the ways of sin and death, and to seek the love of God?

Our egos are the products of our creation under the influence of the world around us. Without God in our minds and hearts we are mostly animals with an intellect that justifies our desires. There is a craving in every human to connect with our Maker, but for a myriad of reasons we hold back from the decision to reach out beyond our limitations and have a loving relationship with God. I have written this autobiography to illustrate some of the ways I have lived which have real consequences beyond this world. There will come a day in my life when I will die, and that will be the day that I am raised up to become the person that God created me to be before the beginning of time. I have experienced life on the

Lessons Learned

mountaintop and in the darkest valley of death. My hope is by sharing this journey you will benefit from my experience. This little life we have been given is very brief and unpredictable. Life in this world can come to an abrupt end at any moment. We have not a minute to waste when it comes to deciding whether we want Jesus to be a partner in our lives. When you experience the love of God in Jesus you will only regret that you waited as long as you did to seek Him. The most startling realization is that he wants to be intimately involved in our lives. No matter what we think of ourselves, He loves us. It is called amazing grace that Jesus is waiting for each of us to turn our life over to Him. Everything He has for us is good. Jesus said in John 8:12 "I am the light of the world. Whoever follows me will never walk in darkness but will have the light of life."

May the light of God be your way, may the Spirit of Christ Jesus be your truth, and may the blessings of God be your life. Everyone who comes to Jesus comes to God.

Lessons Learned

Lessons Learned

1. When we call upon God there will be a response. God wants a relationship with us. Do we have the courage to ask God for help?
2. It is emotionally painful to face ourselves honestly as sinners and accept that we cannot save ourselves. There is no way around the failures in our lives and our complete dependency upon God.
3. We have invested our lives in becoming the persons we created. It is challenging to let go of that creation to become someone different in the image of Jesus Christ.
4. There is a support group for people seeking salvation and transformation. The Christian Church exists for this very purpose and it is waiting for you.
5. The collection of testimonies about who God is, and who we are, is called the Bible. This God-inspired literature has everything we will ever need to know about our relationship to God.